THE PINEAPPLE THEORY

Steve "Mr. Pineapple" Mathieu

The Pineapple Theory

ISBN: 978-1-1777411-8-1

FRUITFUL CONTENTS!

ABOUT THE AUTHOR

Picture by: Anthony "with a camera" Scrocco

Steve *"Mr. Pineapple"* Mathieu is born and raised in Montreal, Canada. French is its native language, and he wrote The Pineapple Theory series in English. He manages Loss Prevention & Safety for 25+ years in retail & supply chain. He is a firm ambassador of Culture and Core Values. When COVID-19 impacted life on Earth, he took full benefit of the forced leisure time sacrifice to reflect – make peace – and become prosperous which trigger its purpose.

S. Mathieu is known for being passionate, for his determination, and for being like the fruit; positively authentic.

The only thing you'll be missing from your reading is Mr. Pineapple's beautiful French-Canadian accent!

Everyone is invited to connect with him on LinkedIn or at: thepineappletheory.ca

"It's all about people with Mr. Pineapple."

- *Readers of The Pineapple Theory*

"Why book readers have not been told fruitful life & leadership principles and sweet perspectives with a pineapple before?"

Steve "Mr. Pineapple" Mathieu

DEDICATION

To you, the reader, make life great because of your greatness.

1

The Seed - Preface

Within you, there's a seed for greatness, cultivate it.

The infamous British *"Soooooory!"* In the United Kingdom, an apology is a golden rule; it's inherited. British culture values heartfelt apologies, both given and received. If you've upset or offended someone, it's important to offer a genuine apology. A half-hearted one won't go down well. It's also common to apologize for things entirely out of one's control. And if you're offered an apology, it's considered good grace to accept it. Refusing may escalate the situation.

Since 2022, I've traveled to London for the annual International Book Fair, a Business-2-Business (B2B) event that became a creative anchor for anything & everything pineapple. My books, my theory, my lens. During photoshoots and video recordings with my pineapple in the city with local photographer Hozir Sahdat from Hozzphoto.com, I've encountered the stretched British *"Soooooory!"* more times than I can count. It's polite. It's performative. It's a mask.

In British culture, *"Soooooory"* often signals a passive-aggressive apology masking intention with grace. It's a *Superego* reflex dressed as social etiquette. And it became the inspiration for this book. Because while the reading journey may taste bitter before it turns sweet, like the tickling effect of a pineapple's first bite, our lives are defined by how we choose to think within. But the voices, the reasoning, the emotions they trigger - are they truly ours?

Everything you know is an illusion. You don't see the world as it is. You see it as your mind wants you to see it. Two people can live at the same moment yet remember completely different realities. Your brain doesn't record the truth, it constructs it. Your perception is not reality. It's a filtered version of it. Every belief you hold, every experience you've had, and every emotion you feel changes how you interpret the world. This is why people argue over facts. Why memories shift over time, and why two individuals can look at the same event and swear it happened differently. If reality is subjective, if the voices, the reasoning, the emotions they trigger – our or not - we can reshape it by changing our inputs, then we change the world surrounding ourselves with new ideas. And perception shifts. Reframe setbacks as opportunities, and our brain will adapt. In the depth of self-acceptance and self-realization, this truth holds, it must be understood with clarity and mastery to influence others. We don't argue with their reality; we reshape how they see it. *Soooooory,* but persuasion isn't about proving; it's about guiding perception. In the end, a person who controls perception controls everything.

In creating *The Pineapple Theory*, I've come to see the crown of the ananas as the mastery of the mind. It means being in full control of our thoughts, shaping the world around us with peace in our eyes because when we are in control of our mind, we are in control of our life. It's never perfect, nor a straight line, but consistency in training the mind is essential. Otherwise, it forgets how.

I've heard people speak as if they know themselves more than they actually do. And that illusion can fade my motivation as an author focused on personal growth. Books? I suggest they're dumbbells for the mind. Because thinking is sacred. Reading books. Having discussions. Pushing our *positive curiosity*. These aren't luxuries; they're lifelines. Your brain isn't a device; it's a temple. And temples don't run on algorithms. They run on awareness.

You'll harvest these truths soon. My theory proposes 15 Fundamental Anchors: the roots of the pineapple. They're timeless, even as we live in time. All research, no matter how advanced, shares conclusions rooted in them. Like your mind, which I call a muscle. Because no matter how far neuroscience evolves - even with AI in the equation - the conclusion remains the same: The less you use your brain, the less it activates. Keep that pace too long, and the mind becomes weak. Not just passive, but dependent. Dependent on what thinks for it, instead of what thinks from it.

In The Pineapple Theory, I offer a warning: As much as technology must evolve, it must never override humanity's ability to think. The same applies to everything inherited, giving blind trust to a pre-built road for our mind. We take it because it's cognitive, it's comfortable. But what do we truly know about it? Most importantly, is it truly you?

Humans want unlimited freedom without awareness about everything inherited. But the truth is it terrifies them when faced with endless possibilities. Their mind freezes. So, they create rules, routines, and even self-sabotage not to break free; but to feel safe. The human brain wasn't built for chaos. In fact, dissonance will fuel human's laziness in their way of thinking if not trained to fight it with ease. Therefore, humans crave structure. Too many options lead to paralysis. (Decision paralysis in psychology). It's why people in strict systems often feel more at peace than those with absolute freedom. The paradox in what feels like peace is they'll envy and hate those who truly break free from what is inherited. *Soooooory,* but comfort zones are just padded cells for the mind.

That's where – in many ways - this book becomes a *"Soooooory"* moment. And the first test is to accept that each chapter will be presented and written differently. Why? Because your life will be defined by your ability to handle uncertainty. Expect the following from your reading: a creative blend of biography for inspiration, psychology for understanding, philosophy for perspective, science for curiosity, fiction for creativity, and self-help for action.

Stories and original 100% human-made (organic) extracts from my authorship journey with The Pineapple Theory will be embedded throughout. Psychology and science will be served like real *"Soooooory"* moments because that's what they are in life: reality showing up. Awareness from sincerely being curious by studying ourselves is a rare treasure. Sadly, many can't manage what facts are versus what they believe. It's *cognitive dissonance* they can't accept or navigate with clarity. Some will call it "psycho shit," thinking they're being played, when in fact, they're confronting the reality of their own engineering. An illusion breaks. The comfort zone is disturbed. A belief cultivated to fill a knowledge gap inherited from surrounding voices becomes chaos.

These *"Soooooory"* moments in life always stem from what we can control: how we speak to ourselves, how we discover ourselves without running away, and how we stay grateful for the pain, because it's strength.

- Life's reality will always expose a truth we choose to ignore.
- Life's reality will always force us to act on what we've postponed.
- Life's reality will always make us hold our head in shame for the wrong we blindly applaud.

There is a way to eliminate fear, build unshakable confidence, stop overthinking, kill bad habits, and learn anything faster. You just need to reprogram your brain through neuroplasticity.

The structure of your brain isn't fixed; it's fluid. With every action and every thought, it strengthens, weakens, or creates new pathways. If you begin learning piano, your movements are clumsy. But with repetition, the brain prunes inefficient paths and reinforces the ones that work. Eventually, you play without thinking. Not because you're robotic, but because your brain has sculpted a new path. That's neuroplasticity in motion.

The same principle applies to fear, confidence, habits, learning, and overthinking. What you constantly do gets wired into your brain, like lifting weights builds muscle. Every time you fear something and avoid it, your brain becomes more fearful. But if you act despite the fear, your brain rewires those paths. Over time, the fear fades.

It's the same with everything. "Fake it till you make it" isn't deception; it's direction. Act as if you were the person you want to become. Soon, your brain will make you that person. Novelty, emotional intensity, and repetition accelerate change.

Another thing to expect from this book, as I'm soul-aging, you'll meet repetition and some lengthy moments. For example, you'll read this again in a different context but know this: life can't be navigated with only one anchor. This book doesn't hold all the solutions, nor everything there is to know about psychology. But it offers equipment for a good workout. And its roots are deep to keep steady when everything feels shaky because in life and by nature, it required shaky for the roots to become steady.

And for everything pineapple, and anything that disturbs your thoughts as you read:

With love,

Sooooory!

2

The 5Ws about you

Built & Know Yourself
Control & Master Yourself
Be Yourself & PineHapply Thrive

Why are you?
What are you?
When are you?
How are you?
Who are you?

In a fast-evolving technological era, life and time blur into illusion, distracting us from ourselves. We live surrounded by smart devices, voice assistants, and anthropomorphic gadgets. Yet despite this hyper-connected age, humans are lonelier than ever. We satisfy our social cravings through screens, but this behavior doesn't meet our deeper need for human contact. Technology must evolve for the right reasons, not to replace thinking, not to erase feeling. Because when data becomes the mirror, we risk mistaking our environment for our identity.

Sooooory, but your smart device won't hug you back. It won't ask how your soul is doing.

It's said that everything starts with "why." But understanding is the root of everything. And with my theory - nurtured from emotional pattern recognition across our timeline - your ability to understand begins with one practice: *positive curiosity*.

To *be positively curious* means to explore with emotional openness. In psychology, this aligns with the *Ideomotor Principle*: actions can be triggered by imagining their sensory consequences. Think positively, and you move positively. In Monsters Inc. (2001), monsters once powered their world by scaring children, until they discovered that laughter generated twice the energy. That's the power of emotional reframing.

From my theory's conclusions, *positive curiosity* is the first step to understanding the 5Ws about you. Because in life, the questions rarely change. The answers do. And if your mindset isn't updated, it becomes the very thing holding you back.

In the Japanese culture, it is said that we have 3 faces:
The first we show the World.
The second we show to friends and family.
Third, we show no one, it is the truest reflection of who we are.

But The Pineapple Theory asks: if the root of a pineapple gives one fruit, why would you have multiple faces?

Biologically, the pineapple is a compound fruit formed from a cluster of hermaphrodite flowers, each self-sterile, yet fused into one sweet whole. The fruitlets communicate through the core. In metaphor: your emotional fruit blooms when your inner parts connect. When you are whole.

If you're *positively curious* about yourself, the 5Ws become a blooming cluster of questions, each one ripening into self-realization. And when fruition is achieved - not by magic beans, but by cultivation - you pineHapply thrive from humble victories. Because self-growth is a continuum. And knowing yourself is the root of everything.

Like Biblical study groups, the book doesn't change, but your experience with it does. Life is suffering. It tests you. And within you, war is unavoidable. Everything you avoid eventually controls you. In your hardest moments, you'll be alone fighting a silent war with your inner warrior. Until you win, expect your efforts to go unnoticed

But here's the good news: when you face adversity, when you swap "Why me?" for "Try me," you free yourself. Every challenge you conquer with your inner warrior shapes you into someone stronger. It keeps your soul unbreakable.

Sooooory, but your ego doesn't care about your growth. It cares about being right.

Society loves a "bad boy." Politicians and corporations' profit from this emotional pattern. But the most rebellious act in a conditioned world - inherited even - is to turn your life around. To thrive as your true self. And it's never too late to reclaim that self.

Be positively curious. And remember: the questions stay the same. The answers evolve.

Ever since childhood, I've had an instinctive urge for expansion. To me, the duty of a quality human is the sincere development of one's potential. And potential isn't locked in the future, it's alive now. It's like walking in the desert: one step forward reveals the path. We're all trying to become better versions of ourselves. But it's not child's play.

We all go through an experimental phase; doing the opposite of what the wise advised. We confuse pleasure with happiness. We act without reflection. It's human nature. But be the *guinea pig*. Because for thousands of years, wise voices have spoken, and few have listened.

When you commit to growth, you become one of those voices. You bridge past experiences with new perspectives. You become a day-to-day *guinea pig* of wisdom. And yes, you won't always be listened to. But growth is always needed. Your inner warrior always battles. Like the streets of Montreal in summer, you are always under construction.

Plato once said: *"Only the dead have seen the end of war."*

In life, everything you give attention to becomes you. Focus on growth, and you grow. Focus on fear, and fear grows. In psychology, this is *Convergence*; the brain's ability to merge sensory inputs into unified perception. It's how we form meaning. And it's why the pineapple, a cluster of fruitlets, becomes a symbol of positivity.

Can you imagine a plant refusing water? Even a cactus needs cultivation. Humans are alike. It's not about lacking knowledge; it's about refusing to acquire it. You can't force a pineapple to ripen. In the 16th century, hot houses were built in the UK to grow pineapples. The climate was unfit. The fruit was limited to the rich.

Sooooory but forced growth isn't fruitful. It's fragile.

In psychology, *Semantic Networking* explains how knowledge is stored: concepts are nodes, linked by relationships. It's how we retrieve meaning. And it's why pineapple analogies work; they trigger positive emotion. The shell looks like a net. Each dot connects. Like your thoughts. Like your memories.

Kids' books and sitcoms do this too. In The Big Bang Theory, Amy uses psychology. Leonard uses Star Wars. They speak in metaphors. They speak to Sheldon's inner child. They *establish similarities.*

Be the farmer. Remove what blocks growth. Stimulate it with the right ingredients. Learning never exhausts the mind. Don't try to remember; understand. Have fun. Because your mind remembers how it felt when it learned something.

Consume knowledge like chocolate milk. Speak to your inner child.

Learning means mistakes. You'll never achieve perfection. And if you think otherwise, *Sooooory,* but that's your foolish ego talking. You can achieve greatness through continuous improvement. In Japanese culture, this is *Kaizen*, transforming habits one step at a time. Like eating a pineapple: one sweet bite at a time.

In psychology, this is the *Butterfly Effect*; small actions create massive outcomes. One negative thought can ruin your day. One positive thought can save it.

Invest in yourself. It's free. But you must actively listen. Self-improvement gives life meaning. It's a gift to yourself, and to the world.

As a life and leadership philosopher, my books aren't about teaching. They're about inspiring curiosity. Like someone guiding you to your seat in a dark theater with a flashlight. The seat was always there. You just needed help seeing it. But here's the paradox; children are afraid in the dark. And adults? They're afraid of the light.

Rumi once said: *"Be patient where you sit in the dark. You wander from room to room hunting for the diamond necklace that is already around your neck."*

Books are silent mentors. And yes, I provoke thought. Because when challenged, humans seek balance. I often tell clients: *"Take time to cultivate the seed for thought. Let's reconnect in a month. I'm curious what you'll have harvested."*

Within you is an inner warrior. A seed for greatness. Cultivating it requires freedom, not limitation. When you observe from all angles, you become open. Like a flower blooming. Like a parachute opening.
Sooooory, but if your parachute isn't open, you'll fall fast. And your ego will bark at

the wrong tree.

Your ego is one of your greatest adversaries. It is misleading. It offends. It creates conflict. A blooming mind doesn't just face others; it faces its own mediocre ego. But sweets don't mean weak. It means resilient. Like a winter flower pushing through snow.

You are always a work in progress. And to improve, you must appear foolish. Dumb questions make geniuses. When someone says, *"I have a stupid question,"* I reply, *"Your stupid question makes you intelligent."*

Socrates said: *"The only true wisdom is in knowing you know nothing."* In fact, life teaches us that:

There's what you know.
There's what you know that you don't know.
There's what you don't know that you don't know.

You cannot live better than in seeking to become better. To know yourself takes a lifetime. And as long as you live, keep learning how to live. Educate your mind, and your heart. Because if not, it's no education.

Be the *guinea pig.* Experience. Learn. Understand. You're not just a doer; you're a teacher through understanding.

In psychology, *Meme Theory* explains how ideas spread through imitation. Monkey see, monkey do. Sometimes, someone guides you with open hands. This book is one of those hands.

And yes, it will be lengthy. Because there's more than one road to the top of the mountain. More than one path to Rome. These anchoring messages are lessons. They engage. They persuade. They define leadership.

You can be the captain of your boat.
The leader of your life.
The superhero of your story.
The farmer of your soul.
The artist of your masterpiece.
The engineer of your functionality.
The Head Chef of your life.

Because the more connected the insights within, the more you thrive in the world.

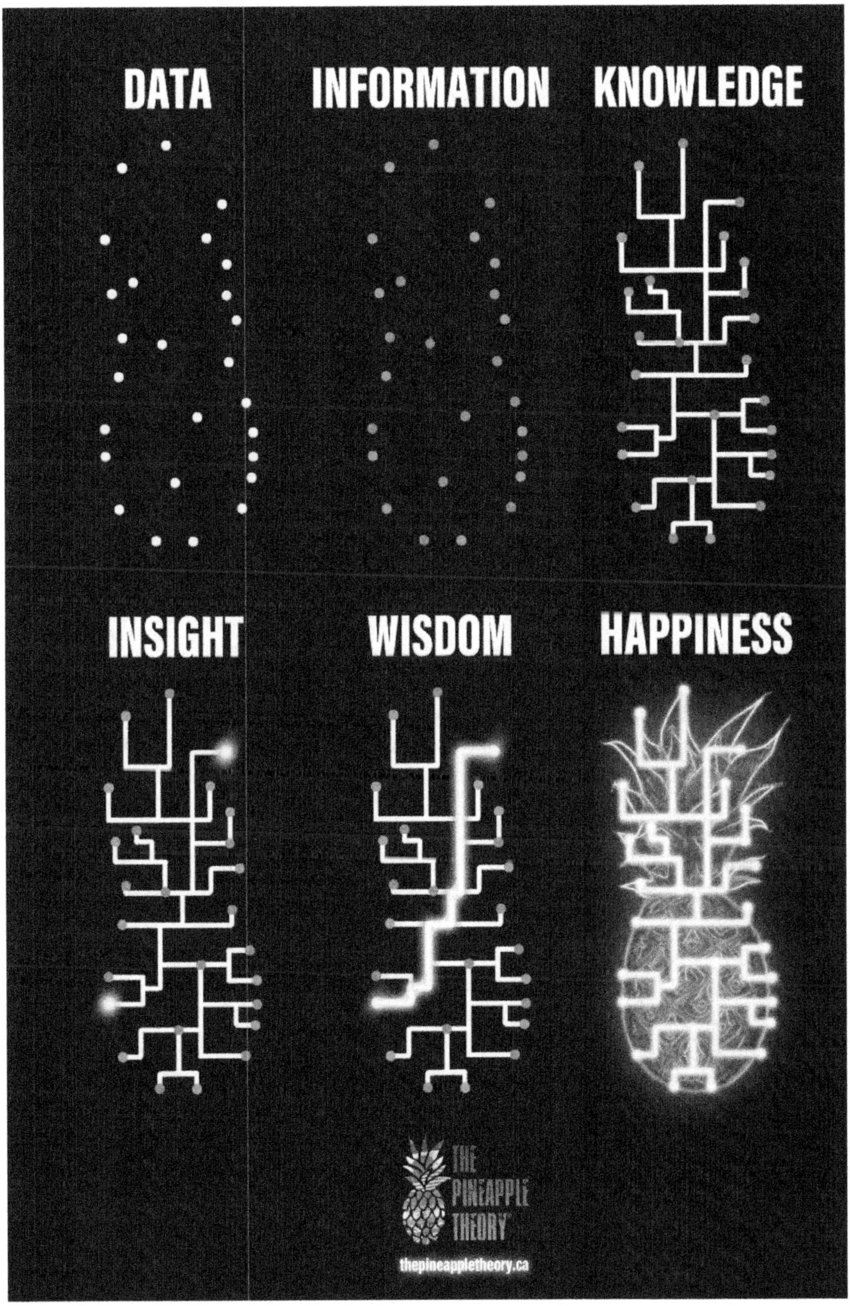
DATA
INFORMATION
KNOWLEDGE
INSIGHT
WISDOM
HAPPINESS
THE PINEAPPLE THEORY
thepineappletheory.ca

Float your boat Captain

Copyright – Steve "Mr. Pineapple" Mathieu – London 2025 - Picture by Hozzphoto.com

What if life was like a river?

To embark on the journey, you need a boat, and you are the captain. In The Pineapple Theory, your boat is a pineapple sliced in half: perfect curve, resilient shell, and a positively authentic bow. Inside, the sweetness, your essence.

Your pineapple boat is your foundation. It keeps you afloat. But it requires maintenance, upgrades, and the right passengers. Because the river doesn't always flow smoothly. Storms will come; some from nature, some from others, some from within.

Soooooory, but not every storm is meant to be weathered head-on. Some require anchoring. Some require pause.

Sometimes, you'll wonder if your boat is Noha's boat, navigating chaos with faith. But storms reveal your craftsmanship. After each one, assess and improve. Because life flows forward. There's no status quo. Your flag must prime in the wind; your compass must stay true.

Your captainship thrives when you actively listen to your crew, when you sweeten the journey for others, and when you keep your pineapple boat floating with grace. Historically, pineapples were used on long voyages to prevent scurvy. Pineapple juice mixed with sand was even used to clean boats.

Sooooory, but if you don't clean your boat, don't complain about the mess.

Starts with you

When we begin our careers, we're like baby pineapples, sweet inside, vulnerable outside. As we mature, protecting that inner sweetness becomes essential. In leadership, it starts with the heart. Craig Groeschel once said: *"People would rather follow a leader with a heart than a leader with a title."*

Titles may be necessary, but they're not sufficient. Leading without authority requires emotional artistry. What if each person was born to be a thriving leader? What if we are all the CEO, COO, and CFO of our lives?

We operate our emotions.
We manage our resources.
We lead our growth.
We establish partnerships.
We define our legacy

Sooooory but blaming others for your life's direction is like blaming the wind for your boat's course.

In organizations, technical mastery often earns promotion. But leadership isn't just technical, it's emotional. The higher you rise, the less it's about you. True leaders consult, include, and inspire. Not everyone will join the journey, especially those anchored in comfort zones. But leadership starts with you, because it's not about you.

Be your own hero

Long ago, humans imagined the *Spiritual Awakening*, a figure seated in meditation, surrounded by the cosmos. Crown Chakra. Third Eye (which resembles a pinecone). Throat. Heart. Solar Plexus. Sacral. Root. When balanced, one returns to their true self. That's the superpower.

Image from Google

Marvel Studios captured this beautifully in Thunderbolts, where unresolved shadows become dangerous. The inner beast, buried too long, awakens. It's not just cinematic, it's psychological. Freud called it the *Shadow Self*, the unconscious part of our psyche that holds the traits we deny, repress, or disown. It's the part we hide from others, and often from ourselves. But buried doesn't mean gone. The Shadow waits. And when ignored, it doesn't disappear, it metastasizes.

That's the brilliance of the Shadow: it reveals what we refuse to see. And that's why self-awareness isn't optional, it's survival. Because if you don't face your Shadow, it will face you. In your relationships. In your reactions. In your silent wars.

Soooooory, but the parts of you you've buried aren't dead because you're always home for your inner demons. They're just waiting for a trigger.

Each superhero reflects a part of us:

Captain America: resilience
Spider-Man: intuition
Dr. Strange: open-mindedness
Moon Knight: inner synergy with the *Shadow Self.*
Hulk: self-control
Shapeshifting Super Skrull: Shaping to life's challenges.
Iron Man: ego transformation
Captain Marvel: identity reclamation
Princess Shuri: healing through truth

Soooooory, but your superpower won't awaken until you stop pretending to be someone else because no one is coming to save you. Become your own hero.

Even the Infinity Stones reflect emotional archetypes:

Mind: discernment
Reality: embodiment
Soul: purpose
Power: action
Space: expansion
Time: presence

They orbit like anchors, each one a force of emotional electricity.

Head Chef

Let's make *Eleutheromania* our word of the day: a manic yearning for freedom. It's not madness, it's a message. A craving to explore, to grow, to taste life fully.

Soooooory, but freedom isn't found in escape. It's found in ownership.

As Head Chef of your life, you choose the ingredients. You refine the recipe. You serve the experience. And yes, I'll ramble again, because flavor takes time to simmer. Like pineapple, sweetness comes from patience, not shortcuts.

You hold the knife, not to harm, but to heal. To cut away what no longer serves your freedom or happiness.

Because salt and sugar look the same, you must taste before you trust. You decide the ratio. You balance the recipe of your life and work, not by default, but by design.

You choose to experiment. Recipes in cookbooks reflect the author's taste, not your truth. If you follow them exactly, you may enjoy the result. But what if the recipe calls for one pineapple ring, and you add two? The outcome becomes a *Schrödinger's Slice*; you might love it, hate it, or feel both. But the point is: you tried. You created. You moved.

Sooooory, but perfection isn't the goal. Participation is.

Everything you make will be tasted by others. Every dish is a reflection of your emotional seasoning. Great chefs don't just feed; they offer an experience. They serve memory, meaning, and metaphor.

And in life, you are the Head Chef. You choose the ingredients. You refine the flavor. You decide what's worth plating, and what's better left uncooked.

Schrödinger's *Sooooory:* The Mirror Paradox

Before moving on to the next chapter, anchor this reflection, it sets the emotional tone for many interpretations throughout this book.

The ironic truth about life is that you are a different person to everyone you meet. To some, you're distant and hard to know. To others, you're the kindest soul they've encountered. Some see you as unforgettable. Others, as a passing thought.
But none of these versions are the real you. They're reflections, mirrors of how others choose to see you. People don't see you as you are; they see you as they are. Their perception of you is shaped by their own emotional landscape. And the same applies to the world around you; it reflects how you choose to see it.

This is the paradox of identity. And it's where *Schrödinger's Sooooory* lives.

It's the apology you offer for being misunderstood, even when you've done nothing wrong. It's the tension between being seen and being distorted. It's the emotional quantum state of being both too much and not enough at the same time.

Sooooory, but you'll never control every reflection.
Sooooory, but someone will always misjudge your light as glare.

No matter what you do, you will always reflect what others need, fear, or expect. And the truth is, no matter how carefully you shape yourself to fit their expectations, someone will still misunderstand you. If you spend your life trying to control how others see you, you'll lose sight of your own reflection.

But maybe real peace doesn't come from being understood by everyone. Maybe it comes from no longer needing to be.
Because the only version of you that truly matters is the one you live with when no one else is watching. The one who doesn't stretch an apology to fit someone else's comfort. The one who doesn't shrink to fit someone else's lens.

That version? That's the pineapple. Whole. Sweet. Unapologetic.

Why are you?
What are you?
When are you?
How are you?
Who are you?

3

The Soil

Never forget yourself
Never lose yourself
Reclaim yourself

The Soil Beneath the Sweetness

Before we descend into the architecture of the mind, let us pause at the threshold.

The Pineapple Theory was born from a simple yet radical question: *What if emotional wisdom had a shape?* What if life and leadership could be cultivated like a fruit; rooted in ancient patterns, sweetened by emotional mastery, and crowned by mental clarity?

To cultivate "pineHapply" people, I studied tens of thousands of years across our human timeline. I traced emotional patterns, inherited beliefs, and psychological rhythms. These became the Fundamental Anchors of the theory, the roots of the pineapple. Then came the inner sweetness: the management of our emotions along with the skin for emotional control. And finally, the Crown: the mastery of our mind. Because where the mind goes, emotions follow.

But over years of refinement, self-education, and lived experience, I realized something was missing. Something foundational. Something invisible yet essential.

I had forgotten the **Soil**.

This chapter is about the Soil, the unseen layer beneath our emotional fruit. It's the ground we stand on, the unconscious terrain that feeds our growth or starves it. Without rich soil, even the strongest roots will wither. Without grounding, even the most radiant Crown will collapse.

The upcoming three hypotheses are not just intellectual ideas. They are emotional excavations. They reveal the hidden forces that shape our beliefs, behaviors, and identity. They expose the Shadow Self, the Superego's borrowed ideals, and the Default Mode Network's autopilot narration. They challenge the reader to step back, not to escape the storm, but to see it clearly.

You will often hear me refer to life and time as an emotional illusion. Not because they aren't real, but because they are often misinterpreted. Like a boat in a storm, we must learn to step back, anchor deep, and observe the waves; not just react to them. That's the Soil. That's where clarity begins.

And *Sooooory*, but these hypotheses may disturb your perspective about who you are in your mind. They may challenge the stories you've inherited, the identities you've constructed, and the beliefs you've never questioned. That's not a flaw. That's the point.

Later in this book, you'll uncover a text titled *Where's Waldo with a Pineapple in the Matrix?* A playful yet piercing metaphor that will echo what begins here. Because sometimes, to find ourselves, we must first lose the mask we didn't know we were wearing.

Following this chapter, you will be presented - imperfectly, perfectly human-made -

through the lens of The Pineapple Theory - a framework woven with rich philosophical and psychological analogies, metaphors, and emotional truths - the roots, the sweetness, the skin, and the Crown. But before we reach the fruit, we must understand the ground. These hypotheses are bridges. They are the checkpoint. They are the invitation to grow with intention, not just momentum.

So, take a breath. Step into the Soil. And let the truth beneath you rise.

Hypothesis 1: The Superego and the Default Mode Network: Reclaiming the Inner

Prelude

"Sooooory!" she said, not because she had harmed, but because she had existed too loudly.

In the museum of the mind, the *Superego* is the docent who whispers, *"Not like that."* It polishes the exhibits of memory, curates the acceptable narratives, and dims the lights on anything too wild, too raw, too real. It is the voice behind the reflexive apology, the one that arises not from guilt, but from inherited shame.

The *Default Mode Network*, that quiet constellation of introspection, is where this docent lives. It activates when we are alone with ourselves, when we rehearse conversations, revise our past, or pre-emptively apologize for futures not yet lived. It is the neural architecture of self-consciousness, and the *Superego* is its most insistent tenant.

But what if the museum could become a temple? What if the apology could become a poem?

Introduction: Two Invisible Forces That Shape Your Mind

This section of the chapter explores a powerful hypothesis: that two seemingly separate psychological forces - the *Superego* and the *Default Mode Network* (DMN) - may be working together to shape your inner life in ways you've never consciously noticed.

The *Superego*, a Freudian concept, is the internalized voice of authority - parents, teachers, religion, society - telling you what's right or wrong, acceptable or shameful.

The *Default Mode Network*, a discovery of modern neuroscience, is the brain's resting-state system; active when you're not focused on the outside world, and deeply involved in self-reflection, moral reasoning, and social comparison.

This section of the chapter proposes that the *Superego* may inhabit the *DMN*. That the moral voice you hear during quiet moments isn't your authentic self, but a script written by others. And that personal growth begins when you learn to rewrite that

script.
We'll begin by exploring each concept in simple terms, then present the hypothesis of their relationship, and finally offer coaching and self-help practices to help you reclaim your inner narrative.

Part I: The Superego — The Voice That Was Never Yours

Freud introduced the *Superego* in his 1923 work *The Ego and the Id*, describing it as the internalized moral authority formed through identification with parental and societal standards. It develops during early childhood, absorbing rules, expectations, and ideals from caregivers, culture, and institutions. Over time, these external voices become internalized, forming what we mistake for our conscience.

But the *Superego* is not your authentic moral compass. It's a system of inherited commands. It rewards conformity with pride. It punishes deviation with guilt and shame.

Philosophically, this echoes Friedrich Nietzsche's critique in *On the Genealogy of Morality*, where he distinguishes between "master morality" (self-defined values) and "slave morality" (values imposed by others). Nietzsche warns that inherited morality - especially religious morality - often suppresses vitality, creativity, and authenticity. In his view, the "good person" is frequently just the obedient one, shaped by fear of divine punishment or social rejection. This moral obedience becomes a spiritual echo within the *Superego*, reinforcing guilt not just socially, but metaphysically.

Psychologically, the *Superego* is linked to *Introjected Regulation*, a form of motivation driven by guilt and obligation rather than personal endorsement (Deci & Ryan, 1985). It's also associated with *Maladaptive Perfectionism*, where individuals strive for unrealistic standards to avoid shame. And in trauma-informed frameworks, the *Superego* can become hyperactive, leading to chronic self-criticism and emotional paralysis.

In coaching, we often see this in clients who feel guilty for resting, selfish for setting boundaries, or anxious when they prioritize their own needs. These are not moral failures; they're symptoms of *Superego* dominance.

This is where *The Pineapple Theory* offers a liberating lens. *Darwin's Theory* - one of the 15 Fundamental Anchors - reminds us that *our environment is us, because we are our environment.* Everything we consume - books, films, conversations, relationships - taints and shapes our personality. The *Superego* is not just built from parental commands; it's reinforced daily by the media we absorb, the networks we engage, and the cultural memes we inherit.

This is why *Meme Theory* becomes so vital. Ideas replicate and manifest within us, often unconsciously. Unless we've broken free from the *Superego*, we remain vessels for inherited scripts, living out values that aren't truly ours.

And this is where *Pavlov's Classical Conditioning* - another Anchor - adds clarity. We are conditioned to associate approval with obedience, and disapproval with deviation. Over time, this creates automatic responses: guilt when we rest, shame when we say no, anxiety when we assert ourselves.

But beneath these layers of conditioning lies the true self. Not the obedient self. Not the performative self. But the self that chooses values consciously, not compulsively. The *Superego* is not evil. It's outdated. And until we update it, we'll keep mistaking obedience for goodness, and guilt for truth.

Part II: The Default Mode Network — The Brain's Storyteller

Discovered through fMRI studies in the late 1990s (Shulman et al., 1997; Raichle et al., 2001), the *Default Mode Network* (DMN) is a constellation of brain regions that activate when we're not focused on the outside world. It's the system behind daydreaming, self-reflection, moral reasoning, and imagining how others perceive us. In short, it's where your mind goes when it's "at rest"—but it's anything but idle.

Let's briefly explore the key regions within the DMN and what they do:

- Medial Prefrontal Cortex (mPFC): Involved in self-evaluation, moral judgment, and understanding others' emotions. It's the seat of your inner critic and your imagined audience.
- Posterior Cingulate Cortex (PCC): Plays a role in autobiographical memory and emotional salience. It helps you reflect on your past and assign meaning to your experiences.
- Precuneus: Associated with visual imagery and self-consciousness. It helps you picture yourself in different scenarios and track your sense of identity.
- Angular Gyrus: Integrates sensory information and language. It helps you narrate your thoughts and make sense of abstract ideas.
- Hippocampus: Supports memory consolidation and emotional learning. It stores the stories you tell yourself about who you are.

Psychologically, the DMN is implicated in disorders of self - such as depression, anxiety, and PTSD - where the internal narrative becomes distorted. Trauma studies show that DMN activity can be disrupted by stress, leading to impaired self-reflection, increased mind-wandering, and a fragmented sense of identity.

Together, these regions form your mind's internal broadcasting system. They construct your self-image, rehearse your social roles, and replay your emotional history. They are the architects of your inner museum.

Philosophically, this echoes William James's "stream of consciousness", a continuous flow of inner experience. It also resonates with Descartes' *Cogito, ergo sum* ("I think, therefore I am"), though modern neuroscience might revise it to: *I narrate, therefore I believe.* Eastern traditions, too, have long emphasized the importance of observing the mind's chatter; Buddhism calls it "monkey mind," and meditation is the practice

of returning to the self beneath the noise.
But here's the question: If the DMN is your mind's storyteller… Who's writing the script?

This is where *The Pineapple Theory* offers a transformative lens. Your mind is your power tool. It connects your roots, stabilizes your foundation, and supervises your emotions. How you care for it - how you train it, speak to it, and recharge it - determines the shape of your authentic pineapple crown.

Psychology tells us that your mind is always searching for proof of what you believe. This is *Confirmation Bias* in action. If you tell yourself that life is hard, your brain will seek out every setback to confirm that narrative. But if you ask, "What good is happening in my life?" Your brain will begin to look for those answers. It will seek out small victories, moments of growth, and opportunities for change. This is the *Law of Balance* at work, another Fundamental Anchor of the Theory.

Your thoughts are your cure, and your placebo. They shape your perception, your habits, and eventually, your actions. In psychology, this is echoed by *Ideomotor Theory*, which suggests that a thought or mental image can trigger automatic muscular reactions, even without conscious intention. Your thoughts become your movements. Your beliefs become your behaviors.

And this is why *Positive Curiosity* is essential, one of the theory's three core Fundamental Anchors, and a power tool of thought designed to interrupt negative emotions triggered by distorted DMN narratives. Per *The Pineapple Theory's* anchors, phrases like "I think," "I assume," "I believe," and "I guess" are cues, not conclusions. They invite us to challenge assumptions, explore ideas, and rewrite inherited scripts. Because if you don't challenge your beliefs, the walls around you grow taller, and logic can no longer be seen. The DMN is where those beliefs live. It's where tired thoughts return to haunt you. It's where emotional illusions masquerade as truth. That's why your mind must be treated as a temple. A sacred space powered by emotional electricity. A place to recharge, not to drain. A museum of your timeline, filled with artifacts, some painful, some proud. Inside this temple, your past is stored in see-through boxes. Not to trap you, but to remind you. To show you how far you've come. To help you return to yourself, not just find yourself.

And just like London's Natural History Museum, where Darwin's legacy and a pineapple plant share space on the ceiling, your temple is a place of science, story, and soul. The fruit is the jewel of the jungle. And your mind is the jewel of your journey. But beware:

The artifacts inside your temple can trick you. They whisper old fears. They replay old guilt. They try to open the door to chaos. You are the bouncer. Your inner warrior guards the gate. And the more Kind, Truthful, Peaceful, and Organized you are within, the more blooming you will attract, speak, and act. So, install the sign. Inside and out.

NO NEGATIVE EMOTIONS ALLOWED.

Because the DMN is not just a network. It's your museum. Your temple. Your story. And you get to decide what's on display.

Part III: The Hypothesis — Superego as DMN's Hidden Director

I suggest the following:

- The Superego *inhabits* the DMN.
- It supplies the moral script.
- The DMN performs it.

This hypothesis is supported by several converging lines of evidence:

- Functional Overlap: Both the *Superego* and DMN are involved in moral reasoning, self-evaluation, and social cognition. Studies show that the medial prefrontal cortex - central to the DMN - is active during moral judgment tasks.
- Developmental Parallels: The *Superego* forms during childhood through social conditioning. The DMN also matures during adolescence, shaping identity and emotional regulation.
- Neuropsychological Correlates. A 2024 study by Chan et al. found that trauma-exposed individuals showed reduced DMN activity in self-referential processing, suggesting that stress can disrupt the internalized moral narrative.
- Ego-Function Research: Sturm (2019) explored neural correlates of Freud's ego functions using resting-state fMRI. The study found correlations between Superego-like traits and DMN connectivity, particularly in the precuneus and medial prefrontal cortex.
- Global Workspace Theory: The DMN may act as a "global workspace" for integrating internal representations. If the *Superego* dominates this workspace, it could shape the entire self-narrative through inherited moral scripts.

This suggests that the *Superego* is not just a psychological construct, it may be a *Neural Director*, scripting your inner life from behind the scenes. And unless you consciously intervene, you can't break free, and you'll live by a story you didn't choose.

Part IV: Coaching & Self-Help Perspectives — Rewriting the Inner Narrative

If the *Superego* influences the DMN, then coaching becomes a form of *Neural Editing*. I help clients identify inherited scripts, challenge them, and rewrite their internal narrative. This is where *The Pineapple Theory* offers clarity. By observing how people respond under stress, we reveal the *Superego*'s grip. By practicing *Positive Curiosity*, I help clients rewire the DMN with self-chosen values. This is not just psychological work; it's neurological liberation.

Practice Exercises: Reclaim Your Inner Voice

Superego Audit
Write down five moral rules you follow without question. For each, ask:
- Who taught me this?
- Does it align with my values today?

DMN Awareness Ritual
During quiet moments (shower, walk, journaling), notice your inner dialogue. Ask: Is this voice mine, or inherited?

Guilt Reframe
Recall a moment you felt guilty for doing something healthy (resting, saying no). Reframe it: What value was I honoring?

Narrative Rewrite
Choose one recurring self-criticism. Rewrite it as a value-driven affirmation. Example: "I'm lazy" → "I'm learning to rest without guilt."

Boundary Practice
Set one boundary this week that feels uncomfortable but necessary. Observe the guilt. Let it pass. Then reflect: Did I feel freer, or more aligned?

Mask Audit
Recall a moment when stress revealed something unexpected about yourself or someone else.
What did you learn? What did it expose about the Superego's influence?

Pineapple Lens Practice
Observe someone under pressure this week. Don't judge; just notice. What does their response reveal about their internal narrative?

Marcus Moment
Each time you face resistance this week, repeat: *"What stands in the way becomes the way."* Let it guide your response, not just your reaction.

Closing Reflection

You are not your conditioning. You are not your guilt. You are not the voice that punishes you for choosing yourself. You are the author of your inner narrative. And the moment you reclaim that pen, the DMN becomes your canvas, not your cage.

This chapter stands as a bridge, anchoring the chapters that came before, and illuminating the path for those that follow. Because in life, Freedom, Peace, Love, Respect, Kindness, good manners, and good etiquettes are not random gifts. They are cultivated from how we speak to ourselves. They are shaped by our embodied values and protected by our established boundaries.

So, rewrite. Reframe. Reclaim. Because freedom isn't found in silence. It's found in the courage to speak with your own voice.

Hypothesis 2: The Science and Faith Coexistence Hypothesis

Where logic meets belief, and peace begins.

Prelude

"SOOOOORY!" she whispered; not because she had sinned, but because she had dared to ask, *"What if?"*

This hypothesis is not just *Soooooy*. It's a ***SOOOOORY,*** a moment of emotional electricity. A confrontation with inherited belief. A call to logic, not to replace faith, but to coexist with it.

Introduction: Belief as Comfort, Not Conflict

This chapter complements the Belief Anchor of *The Pineapple Theory*. It does not seek to dismantle faith, but to honor its emotional function. Because belief, for many, is comfort. It's a form of positive affirmation. It soothes anxiety, recharges emotional batteries, and offers meaning in the face of uncertainty.

But when belief becomes blind, it builds walls. And when logic is exiled, peace with our neighbor becomes impossible. The *Superego* and the DMN walk hand-in-hand through inherited belief. They script our moral reflexes, our emotional reactions, and our spiritual obedience. But what if we could rewrite the script?

Story from the Field: Coaching with the Extreme Obvious

In 2018, in Mexico, a priest made headlines - and a fortune - by selling plots of land in heaven for $100. He claimed divine approval from a private meeting with God in 2017. This story is extracted from my book *Worldwide Fruitful Travels with a Pineapple*, and it's what I call *coaching with the extreme obvious*; a moment where belief overrides logic, and obedience becomes exploitation.

It's also a disguise marketing tactic: selling salvation as a product, monetizing faith through emotional manipulation. And it's not an isolated case. It's a pattern.

Part I: The Hypothesis - Belief as a Gap-Filler

What was there before nothing?

This question activates several Fundamental Anchors from *The Pineapple Theory*: Curiosity Gap, Classical Conditioning, Belief, Laziness, Cue Words for Reasoning, and Positive Curiosity.

Inherited belief often answers: "God." Not from logic, but from emotional necessity.

It's the **God of the gaps**, a placeholder for the unknown.

Historically, this pattern repeats. In 150 AD, Claudius Ptolemy, observing planetary motion, wrote:

"When I trace the windings of the heavenly bodies, I no longer touch Earth. I stand in the presence of Zeus."

He didn't understand the planets, so he invoked deity. Today, we know why planets move. Newton and Kepler filled that gap. But new gaps remain. And when science hasn't yet threaded the needle, belief steps in.

Hypothesis

Where science has not yet reached, belief becomes the answer. And when belief is inherited without logic, it becomes an ever-receding pocket of ignorance. Not because faith is wrong, but because it's used to silence curiosity.

As Bertrand Russell warned, *"The whole problem with the world is that fools and fanatics are always so certain of themselves, and wiser people so full of doubts."*

And Nietzsche cautioned that inherited morality often suppresses vitality, creativity, and authenticity, turning obedience into a false virtue.

Part II: Psychological Lens — Untangling the Mind of Belief

Belief is not just spiritual; it's neurological, emotional, and social. Let's explore the architecture:

- **Superego & DMN Convergence**: The *Superego* scripts inherited moral codes. The DMN replays those codes as emotional truth. Together, they create a loop of obedience, guilt, and self-justification.
- **Authority Principle (Milgram, 1963)**: People obey perceived authority, even when it contradicts logic or ethics. When "God" is invoked by leaders, it amplifies obedience and suppresses critical thinking. This is especially dangerous when leaders construct their own "truth" from lies, and *Meme Theory* helps those lies replicate faster than facts.
- **Meme Theory (Dawkins, 1976)**: Beliefs replicate like viruses; through imitation, repetition, and emotional resonance. Even when disproved by data, memes persist if they serve emotional or tribal identity.
- **Confirmation Bias**: The brain seeks evidence to support existing beliefs. Contradictory data is ignored, rationalized, or attacked. This is why belief systems often resist correction, even when the facts are clear.
- **Cognitive Dissonance (Festinger, 1957)**: When belief and logic collide, discomfort arises. To reduce dissonance, people often reject logic rather than revise belief.

- **Continued Influence Effect**: Even after misinformation is corrected, it continues to shape perception. People create auxiliary explanations to preserve their worldview.
- **Emotional Batteries**: Belief recharges emotional energy. But blind belief can short-circuit logic, leading to dependency and manipulation.
- **Neuroplasticity**: Beliefs are not fixed; they're wired through repetition. Challenging belief rewires the brain but requires emotional safety and cognitive effort.

And here's the emotional truth: Belief, when inherited without logic, becomes a cognitive fortress protecting comfort but resisting truth.

Part III: Coaching & Self-Help Perspectives — Rewiring the Mind

If belief fills the gaps, coaching becomes a form of mental scaffolding, supporting the transition from blind obedience to conscious understanding.

Practice Exercises

1. Belief Audit

Write down five beliefs you hold about life, death, or purpose. For each, ask:

- Who taught me this?
- Does it align with my values today?
- Is it emotionally comforting or logically sound; or both?

2. Cue Word Reframe

Notice when you say: "I think," "I believe," "I assume." Pause. Ask:

- Is this a conclusion or a question?
- What data supports it?
- What emotion is attached to it?

3. Authority Check

Recall a moment when someone invoked "God," "Truth," or "Leadership" to justify a claim. Ask:

- Was it backed by logic or emotion?
- Did it invite curiosity or demand obedience?
- If the belief or "truth statement" was disproven by data, did I reject it or accept it? And why?

4. Narrative Rewrite

Choose one inherited belief that causes guilt or fear. Reframe the question; rewrite it as a value-driven affirmation. Example: "If I question God, I'll be punished." → "Curiosity is how I honor the divine."

5. Boundary Practice

Set one boundary this week that challenges inherited belief. Observe the emotional reaction. Let the guilt pass. Reflect: Did I feel freer, or more aligned?

6. Pineapple Lens Practice

Observe someone invoking belief to justify behavior. Don't judge, just notice. What does it reveal about their emotional architecture?

7. Marcus Moment

Each time you face resistance this week, repeat: *"What stands in the way becomes the way."* Let it guide your response, not just your reaction.

Closing Reflection

You are not your conditioning. You are not your guilt. You are not the voice that punishes you for asking questions. You are the author of your inner narrative. And the moment you reclaim that pen, belief becomes a bridge, not a wall.

Faith and science are not enemies. They are languages. And peace begins when we learn to speak both.

Soooooory, but belief without logic is not peace. It's paralysis. So, rewrite. Reframe. Reclaim. Because freedom isn't found in silence. It's found in the courage to think, feel, and ask; *What if?*

Hypothesis 3: The Shadow Self Hijack Hypothesis

When suppression becomes sabotage, and peace begins with integration.

Prelude

"Soooooory," he said, not because he had hurt someone, but because he had finally seen the part of himself, he'd spent years hiding.

This hypothesis is not just *Soooooory.* It's a mirror. A confrontation with the parts of ourselves we exile to be loved, accepted, and rewarded. It's a call to make peace with the war inside.

Introduction: The Shadow Isn't Evil - It's Unseen

This third hypothesis continues our exploration of the hidden forces that shape our inner life. It invites readers into one of the most profound confrontations of all: the moment we stop running from ourselves.

The *Shadow Self,* as described by Carl Jung, is not just a psychological blind spot, it's a force that, when suppressed, can hijack the Default Mode Network (DMN) and distort our inner narrative. The *Superego,* in its quest for moral perfection, tempts us to suppress traits deemed unacceptable rather than understanding them: rage, envy, ego, lust for control. But what we exile doesn't vanish. It becomes autonomous.

Over time, it leaks into our lives through passive aggression, addiction, self-sabotage, and emotional volatility. The *Shadow Self* then becomes the narrator of our mind - often negatively - and it's the *Ideomotor Principle* in motion: our thoughts become our actions, even when we don't realize it.

Sooooory, you call yourself a good person, but that's *Identity Naming* in psychology. In reality, you may simply be someone who's learned to hide your darker traits well. But the more you suppress them, the louder they scream. And eventually, they will take control.

Even comedy knows the cost. In Seinfeld (S9E3), it's Lloyd Braun - George's childhood neighbor - who warns, *"Serenity now… insanity later."* Kramer, who adopts the mantra to suppress his emotions, eventually breaks down in a fit of rage. It's a perfect metaphor for the *Shadow Self:* what we suppress doesn't disappear; it waits.

And in The Simpsons (S13E18), it's Homer's transformation into *Angry Dad,* a web cartoon character born from his own repressed rage. What begins as a joke becomes a mirror. Homer's emotional outbursts, once hidden behind denial and distraction, erupt into exaggerated caricature. The more he ignores his anger, the more it defines him. *Angry Dad* isn't just a cartoon, it's Homer's Shadow, animated.

This hypothesis is not here to shame. It's here to liberate. Because peace doesn't come from perfection, it comes from integration. And only unified minds can evolve, like clusters of flowers forming the pineapple fruit, in the right environment.

The Hypothesis — Shadow as DMN Hijacker

Carl Jung warned: *"Until you make the unconscious conscious, it will direct your life, and you will call it fate."*

What people often call fate is not destiny; it's emotional inertia. It's the *Shadow Self* acting out suppressed desires, wounds, and instincts. It's *Superego* enforcing inherited beliefs that were never questioned. It's the DMN replaying emotional scripts written by others.

The *Superego*'s ego-ideal is not your ideal. It's a borrowed standard; constructed from external voices, shaped by culture, religion, and authority. It rewards conformity, not clarity. It punishes deviation, not dishonesty. And when we mistake it for our true self, we suppress the parts that don't fit the mold. That's where the Shadow begins to form.

Childhood Emotional Neglect (CEN) is one of the most common roots of Shadow formation. When a child's emotional needs are unmet - not through abuse, but through absence - they learn to suppress their feelings to maintain connection. Over time, these disowned emotions are absorbed into the Shadow. The *Superego* then moralizes this suppression, and the DMN replays it as identity. Adults shaped by CEN often feel guilty for needing rest, ashamed of their emotions, or afraid to express vulnerability. But these are not flaws, they are echoes of a childhood where silence felt safer than selfhood

Internalized Emotional Regulation, especially in the form of emotional withdrawal, often begins as suppression, but with time, it becomes a deeper disengagement. The inner child learns to silence feelings not just to be accepted, but to survive. In adulthood, this pattern is common among business executives, entrepreneurs, and emotionally attuned leaders. They are told "no" often. They face rejection, pressure, and expectation. To stay focused, they learn to regulate emotion internally, sometimes at the cost of connection. Even authors, like the one holding this pineapple, experiences emotional withdrawal while still coaching others through theirs. This paradox - emotional leadership through emotional silence - is both a strength and a signal. It deserves compassion, not judgment.

Alexithymia, often misunderstood as emotional absence, is frequently a mask shaped by time. In the context of CEN and internalized regulation, it becomes a survival strategy. The child who suppresses emotion to stay safe eventually loses the language for those emotions. Adults shaped by this pattern may appear stoic, focused, or emotionally detached, but beneath the mask is a sensitive inner child who learned that vulnerability was dangerous. *Alexithymia* is not a flaw, it's a signal. And with time, safety, and integration, the mask can be gently removed.

Hypothesis

The *Superego* tempts suppression.
The *Shadow Self* absorbs what's suppressed.
And when unconscious, the *Shadow* hijacks the DMN, blinding us with emotional distortion until integration becomes the only path to peace.

Problems are not walls to climb over. They are doors to walk through. With courage and kindness. Only then will peace begin to follow you instead of pain.

Psychological Lens — The Architecture of Suppression

Jungian Shadow Theory
The Shadow contains repressed traits, often formed in childhood when we learn what's "acceptable." It includes both negative and positive qualities we've disowned.

Childhood Emotional Neglect (CEN)
Emotional absence teaches children to suppress their needs to preserve attachment. These suppressed traits become the foundation of the Shadow. Adults shaped by CEN often struggle with self-worth, emotional expression, and internal permission

to feel.

Internalized Emotional Regulation
This often begins as suppression, but over time, it escalates into emotional withdrawal. The emotional system shuts down not just to avoid rejection, but because it no longer knows how to feel. In high-functioning adults, this often appears as stoicism or emotional focus. But beneath the surface is often a quiet ache for connection.

Alexithymia as a Time-Shaped Mask
When emotional suppression becomes chronic, the ability to name and feel emotions fades. Alexithymia is not emotional absence; it's emotional amnesia. And it can be unlearned.

Superego Influence
The Superego enforces moral ideals. It tempts suppression by rewarding obedience and punishing deviation. It creates the illusion of goodness through denial.

DMN Vulnerability
The DMN, responsible for self-reflection and emotional narrative, becomes vulnerable when the Shadow is unconscious. Emotional triggers activate suppressed traits, distorting perception and behavior.

Projection & Self-Sabotage
Suppressed traits often manifest as projection, blaming others for what we refuse to see in ourselves. This leads to interpersonal conflict, addiction, and emotional instability.

Ideomotor Principle
Thoughts and mental images can trigger automatic behaviors. Suppressed emotions become unconscious actions - rage, withdrawal, sabotage - without conscious intent.

Neuroplasticity & Emotional Energy
Suppression consumes energy. The more we fight ourselves, the less energy we have for growth. Integration frees emotional bandwidth and rewires the brain toward balance.

Trauma & Attachment
Shadow traits often stem from unmet emotional needs. When ignored, they manifest as attachment dysfunction, resentment, and chronic dissatisfaction.

Belief, when inherited without logic, becomes a cognitive fortress, protecting comfort but resisting truth. The same applies to identity. When we suppress parts of ourselves to fit an ideal, we lose access to our full potential.

Coaching & Self-Help Perspectives — Integration as Liberation

If the Shadow hijacks the DMN, coaching becomes a form of emotional integration, helping clients trace their darkness to its roots, name its parts, and channel its energy toward purpose.

Practice Exercises

1. **Shadow Inventory**

   Write down five traits you dislike in others. Ask:
   - Do I carry these traits in some form?
   - When did I learn to suppress them?
   - What would happen if I acknowledged them?

2. **Emotional Leak Audit**

   Recall a moment of emotional overreaction. Ask:
   - What part of me was triggered?
   - Was it anger, envy, fear, or shame?
   - What suppressed need was trying to speak?

3. **Projection Check**

   Notice when you criticize someone strongly. Ask:
   - Is this trait something I've disowned in myself?
   - If the behavior reflects me, what am I avoiding?
   - If the belief or "truth statement" was disproven by data, did I reject it or accept it? And why?

4. **Narrative Rewrite**

   Choose one suppressed trait. Reframe the question; rewrite it as a value-driven affirmation. Example: "I'm too aggressive." → "I'm learning to channel my assertiveness into leadership."

5. **Integration Practice**

   Use your Shadow consciously.
   - Channel aggression into sport.
   - Use envy to identify unmet desires.
   - Transform vanity into artistic expression.
   - Read books on philosophy and psychology to prevent the Superego, DMN, and Shadow from living free on autopilot.

- Practice meditation or breathwork to observe your emotional patterns without judgment, this builds the muscle of integration.

6. **Pineapple Lens Practice**

Observe someone under stress. Ask:

- What part of their Shadow is surfacing?
- What does it reveal about their emotional architecture?
- If they were raised with emotional neglect, what survival traits might be speaking through their silence?

7. **Marcus Moment**

Each time you feel triggered this week, repeat: *"What stands in the way becomes the way."* Let it guide your integration, not your suppression.

Final Conclusion: The Shadow Isn't Your Enemy - It's Your Echo

You were never broken. You were just divided; split between the self you show and the self you suppress. But the Shadow isn't your enemy. It's your echo. It repeats what you've refused to hear. It acts when you refuse to feel. It hijacks when you refuse to integrate. So don't just chase serenity, trace the scream beneath it. Don't just name your goals, name the parts of you that sabotage them. Because the war inside you isn't meant to be won. It's meant to be ended. And only when you stop rejecting your darkness can your light stop burning out. Study your Shadow, not to silence it, but to speak with it. To walk beside it. To lead with it. Because only unified minds can evolve. And only integrated souls can lead.

4

Perfection is a Myth
There's no perfect pineapple

Thriving with peace is not found in the pursuit of perfection, but in the acceptance of the imperfect.

Montreal's Olympic Stadium: The Beauty of Incompletion

I'm from Montreal, a metropolitan city that bloomed from the late 60's throughout the 70's, and the Montreal Olympic Stadium speaks of life with its unique history.

The locals are calling the Olympic Stadium the giant curling rock, the giant household dry iron, even the spaceship.

In 1976, Montreal hosted the summer Olympics, an event for which each Country hosting the Olympics spent – others will say it's an investment - tons of money for cleaning their city and building new infrastructures to make the city a place people will want to come back to. The Olympic Stadium was one of those infrastructures, an ambitious project with several controversies.

The Olympics – known today – is an event for which all eyes of the world are watching, and the amazing story about the Montreal Olympic Stadium is as follows:

Portions of the stadium, and the full tower, were unfinished and still under construction at the opening ceremonies and for the duration of the games. Yes, the world saw Montreal with a non-completed project.

Today, it may still be a heated topic for society, the media, and politicians, but the Montreal Olympic Stadium is a symbol and a building like no other in the World.

The Montreal Olympic Stadium speaks of life as follows: Investing in yourself always opens doors to new opportunities. The profits take time, you will experience events for which you are not yet ready to present yourself at your best, but you must keep investing and building yourself until completion followed by maintenance, and upgrades.

London Underground: Watch Your Step

It sounds heavy, it's shaky, and it rolls loudly. Yes, it's the notorious London Underground. A symbol, an emblem, and what was an inspiration for several countries who desired to build their own underground train, metro, or subway based on the naming that floats their boat.

From 2022, I travel to London annually to exhibit at the London Book Fair, and the city also inspires several insights for my books. If I had to stay in London, I would not need a vehicle because the Underground truly takes you everywhere. It's the same with Hong Kong, Tokyo, New York, and Frankfurt's underground trains.

The London Underground inspires me because it also isn't perfect. Its history dates to 1863 as the world's first underground railroad, and when using it today, you must watch your step.

Where it's home for me, in Montreal, such an imperfect gap between the flat and train would create an emotional blur with the media becoming society. In London, who cares because everyone knows it's like that, and people are familiar with the gaps. They watch their step like we must all alertly watch our steps in life. Like making usage of our thousand eyes per my kids' book, *The Legend of the Thousand Eyes Pina the Ananas.*

The beauty of what is imperfect about London's Underground is; it takes you safely where you need to go, and that's what truly matters.

Tower of Pisa: Leaning into Life

The city of Pisa, in Tuscany, a region in west-central Italy. On its grounds is the city's cathedral complex, a beautiful white leaning masterpiece called Tower of Pisa.

Known as the Campo dei Miracoli or Piazza dei Miracoli, meaning the Square of Miracles, the leaning architecture marvel can be considered a miracle, not a miracle, or both!

Construction for this imperfect beauty began in the 12th century. The soft ground was unable to support the tower's weight, and the lean worsened as construction progressed and was completed in the 14th century. By 1990, the tower leaned at a 5.5-degree angle and a stabilization project began in 1990, reducing the lean by 15 inches, and the tower has continued to straighten since 2001 and is forecast to remain stabilized for at least 200 years. Highly photographed and playful for tourists, the leaning Tower of Pisa speaks of life as follows.

In life, before building walls, build a foundation, make sure it's solid and that it remains solid. In the process, there will be failures but to thrive in life, you must accept failing. Then, when surrounded with the right people, when you can't stand as straight as usual, the right people will be there for you because it's when you are poor and feeling broken that the right people show up in your life.

Peggy the Pug: Ugly Wins

British Pugese Peggy won Britain's ugliest dog competition and is the star in Marvel's 2024 movie, Deadpool 3, and life is again spoken as follows.

Peggy won an ugly contest and is now an applaud beauty which was influentially conditioned when repeatedly placed into a caring and loving environment for which, Peggy in framed in the environment.

What is perfection?

Applied by several companies is *Lean Six Sigma*, and per its methodology, the closest to perfection is 3.4 defects per million opportunities. If something looks perfect, like the successful launch of a space shuttle, it failed several times prior to its official launch. Also, perfection that led to victory will often not serve you for your new victory, but only by always improving and nurtured from its evolving environment.

Lastly, in science, the x_i symbol suggest *imperfect symmetry*, meaning a small deviation from symmetry which is abundant in nature, but not common among engineering structures. Although, a group of scientists investigated and confirmed whether, and under which conditions the response of engineering structures with given symmetry group Γ may be *improved* by adding small perturbations x_i to the geometry. In fact, they have demonstrated that a naturally emerging representation of Γ in the space of the variable's $\{x_i\}$ plays a key role based on this representation, with exact conditions of improvability, and by utilizing classical representation theory of finite groups.

Through Earth timeline, Prophets, Spiritual Guides, Philosophers, Poets, and more have spoken and wrote a growth continuum that in life, there's no emotional perfection, including proverbs from the world.

Buddha
Better it is to live one day seeing the rise and fall of things than to live a hundred years without ever seeing the rise and fall of things.

Albert Einstein
Anyone who has never made a mistake has never tried anything new.

Mr. Pineapple
Like pineapples on a pizza, keep it sweet with yourself and others because not everything is for everyone. Even pineapples don't stand perfectly straight.

Wa-bi Sa-bi
Japanese meaning: Finding beauty in the imperfections and the impermanence of things.

German proverb
Crooked logs also make straight fires.

African proverb
A beautiful thing is never perfect.

In psychology, *The Pratfall Effect* suggests that individuals, particularly those perceived as highly competent, become more likable and attractive when they make a small mistake or "pratfall".

In life, to be considered highly competent, or an expert to be more accurate, is from the result of making likely all possible mistakes becoming leverage and *guinea pig* experiences speaking value about *The Pratfall Effect* as follow:

This counterintuitive phenomenon can be explained by the fact that it humanizes those who were previously seen as almost superhuman. By revealing imperfections, they become more relatable and approachable, thus increasing their likability.

In one study, researchers compared participants in two job interviews. Same competent candidate, same answers. The only difference in one version is that the participant spilled coffee at the end. That tiny slip made people more likely to hire them. The flaw didn't hurt the interviewee, and study revealed that when competence is already clear, humans beat perfectly.

Publishing Biases: Pineapple vs. Perfection

Throughout Earth timeline, the commercial book industry established & influenced frugal conditioning with how books should be written and presented, feeding an emotional perfection that does not exist. A blur of biases around becoming one of several inner battles to keep my pineapple balance on my inner foundation.

When shopping for pineapple fruit, the fruit's positive authenticity does not stop a customer. When shopping for a book, The Pineapple Theory (TPT) book series are intended to be like pineapples on shelves, meaning like what is a pineapple fruit – positively, authentically, and unapologetically *Soooooory-* standing tall in a mixed plate of fruits making all the other fruits look much more fruitful. The big difference is that the pineapple positive authenticity is known & admired since the 17th century, and TPT, still new, since 2020. Years at swimming counter flow which was one of several inspirations for my text titled: *The determination of a salmon.*

The pineapple's 17th century high-level context is as follows. History suggests that it was Christopher Columbus who brought the pineapple to Europe. Records reveal that in 1493, the friendly inhabitants of the Antilles Island of Guadeloupe welcomed the foreign traveler with this exotic fruit. Columbus was so enamored with its taste that he took it home with him.

In addition to serving as food, with its natural sweetness, the pineapple has served in history as a symbol and an artistic motif. According to *Levins (2004),* the rarity, reputation, expense, and visual attractiveness of the pineapple made it an item of celebrity and the "ultimate exotic fruit." The pineapple was so coveted and uncommon that in 1677, King Charles II of England posed receiving a pineapple as a gift in an official portrait, a symbolic act viewed of royal privilege.

Copyright: Steve "Mr. Pineapple" Mathieu, picture by Olga Tjukova, Dunmore's Pineapple, Scotland

The pineapple became a symbol of hospitality and served as the pinnacle of an entertaining household's feast, even being rented to households during the day for display on the table and then sold to more affluent clients who ate it *(Levins 2004)*. As a symbol of hospitality and friendship, the pineapple became a favorite motif of architects, artisans, and craftsman in the American colonies, and would be seen on the main gate posts of mansions, in the weathervanes of public buildings, and on walls, canvas mats, tablecloths, napkins, the backs of chairs, and so forth *(Levins 2004)*. Even St-Paul's did not escape it, and if you visit London, take quality time to observe the two golden pineapples shining high.

If you are an avid book reader, do expect the writing style of my books – like several chapters of this book - to disturb your comfort zone because it serves as a reminder about what we must experience in life; learning to become comfortable with what is uncomfortable. And like what is interacting with people, it nurtures the value of keeping focus on the messages rather than beauty because that's where the sweetness is found, under the surface. In fact, one pure heart is more beautiful than 1,000 pretty faces. Meaning that I'm fully aware my books manuscripts are not emotionally perfect for everyone, and it is intentional. Like pineapples on a pizza, not everything is for everyone – therefore – one must keep it sweet inside/out with themselves and others.

Because life thrives with patterns, my books also have patterns, like variants of this text, or my books assembled with improved pieces of Legos with the purpose of breaking readers' biases with an industry boxed expectation felt like bullying.

Imagine one voicing "MOOstache" instead of moustache. One has the choice to understand or to voluntarily not understand even if they do. An honest mistake that could be an awareness about one's moustache has a nose booger!

One of several messages shared with my books is that in life, there is no emotional perfection. Per the *Lean Six Sigma* methodology shared earlier, expect 3.4 defects per million opportunities and if something feels perfect, it likely failed several times.

The reading of my books must focus on the messages, not with the bias of "how it's written" resulting in turning down a positive purpose. Ones' bias is one seeking around instead of within.

The positive win over my inner battle with the following mindset nurtured from life's *Law of Balance:* When life gives you lemons, defined as a negative force, I sell them, and I purchase a pineapple.

When potential readers, agencies, and publishers choose turning down a purpose to only encourage what is an emotional perfection from their emotional point of view, it is what it is. I will find my way like I do because in life, there's no gain without pain and you must Believe to Achieve.

One reading my books must read, read, and read again what each book shares to cultivate their thriving growth within. It follows the following wisdom from our history:

Socrates
Employ your time in improving yourself by other men's writings so that you shall come easily by what others have labored hard for.

Plato
Writing is the geometry of the soul.

Epictetus
Don't just say you have read books. Show that through them you have learned to think better, to be a more discriminating and reflective person.

In the emotional illusions with *life & time*, when one's blur of biases is their roadblock, one is walking around with a nose booger on their MOOstache! *Soooooory!*

Be positively curious and when reading this book, you will thrive if you read, think, and relate with the purpose of cultivating your seed for greatness. In the next chapter – the roots – my theory's 15 Fundamental Anchors will be shared "The Pineapple Theory" way, similar to this chapter. But first, here's a zest of practical psychology about perfectionism.

Psychological lens - Why perfectionism isn't discipline; it's fear in disguise.

Perfectionism isn't a virtue. It's a defense mechanism dressed in ambition. Beneath its polished surface lies a fear of rejection, a shame-conditioned belief that says: *"If I make a mistake, I'll lose love, respect, or safety."*

According to *schema therapy* and *cognitive models of perfectionism* (Flett & Hewitt, 2002), this belief often forms in childhood environments where worth was contingent on achievement. The brain encodes this through associative learning:

mistake → criticism → shame.

Over time, the child learns not to strive, but to freeze. Not to express, but to edit. Not to grow, but to hide.

Neuroscientifically, this avoidance is reinforced by hyperactivation in the anterior cingulate cortex (ACC) and amygdala, regions responsible for error detection and emotional threat. The fear of "being seen trying and failing" activates the same circuitry as physical danger. So, the perfectionist doesn't chase excellence. They chase invisibility.

And yet, the paradox is this:

The more we chase perfection, the less we allow ourselves to improve. Because improvement requires imperfection. It requires feedback, failure, and emotional exposure.

This is where *Impostor Syndrome* often joins the party. The perfectionist may appear competent, but inside they feel fraudulent, terrified that one slip will reveal their unworthiness. They overprepare, overperform, and overthink. But they rarely feel safe.

Sooooory, but here's a rambling. Enter the *Pratfall Effect.* Psychological studies show that highly competent individuals become more likable when they make small mistakes. Why? Because it humanizes them. It breaks the illusion of perfection and invites connection. In one study, a candidate who spilled coffee during an interview was rated more favorably than the same candidate who didn't. The flaw didn't hurt them, it helped.

This is the emotional truth: When competence is clear, human beats perfect.

And finally, *Self-Compassion Theory* (Neff, 2003) offers the antidote. It teaches that growth doesn't come from harsh self-judgment, but from kindness, mindfulness, and shared humanity. When we treat ourselves like someone we love, we stop fearing imperfection and start learning from it.

So, what's the coaching proposal? Deliberate imperfection.

Complete a task at 70%. Send the email with one typo. Speak before you're fully ready. Then observe: Did the world end? Did your worth collapse?

This is *exposure therapy* for the perfectionist mind. It creates prediction error, a mismatch between the feared outcome and the actual result. Over time, the brain rewires. The shame-conditioned schema weakens. And the soul begins to breathe. Because real confidence isn't the absence of flaws. It's the presence of action despite them. It's the pineapple standing tall; sweet inside, imperfect outside, unapologetically *Sooooory.*

5

The Roots
15 Fundamental Anchors

Before its branches reach for the sky, its roots push through the darkness, finding stability beneath the surface. The stronger the roots, the taller the tree.

Philosophically, this chapter begins with a revelation: our timeline is not linear; it's a looping continuum. Events repeat in modernized forms, interrupted by painful transition gaps. It's like moving the masses from Ancient Egypt across the Red Sea or reinventing the wheel again and again. This view of reality is not just poetic; it's practical. It invites us to be *positively curious* with our past to better navigate the present.

This philosophy became a Big Bang moment for The Pineapple Theory: *What was, still is.* Human emotions are not just felt; they are built. And life and time? They are emotional illusions.

This echoes Karma's *Law of Connection*, suggesting that past, present, and future are all emotionally linked. It's a view shared by ancient myths and mythologies, written by the wise ones of our past, now their legacy.

Since 2020, I've cultivated The Pineapple Theory by studying the history of the pineapple and harvesting analogies that serve modern coaching. Like a pineapple lamp or plug-in night light, the fruit becomes a symbol of illumination, guiding us through emotional darkness.

People's reactions when learning something new reveal a pattern: Bareness before brilliance. It's the moment when the mind lights up, and the soul says, "I see."

This is the power of pattern disruptors, those who shake the apple tree and plant pineapples instead. In psychology, it's called the *Von Restorff Effect.* When something stands out, it becomes unforgettable.

At book fairs, people ask, *"What's your name?"* I say, *"I'm Mr. Pineapple."* They laugh. Pause. Then ask, *"But what's your real name?"* And I say, *"Mr. Pineapple is what you'll truly remember."*

Why? Because human memory isn't neutral. It's biased toward what breaks the pattern. Distinct stimuli activate the hippocampus and amygdala; regions linked to novelty and emotional salience. Your brain flags the unusual as important. That's why scandals dominate headlines and why pineapples stand tall in a mixed plate of fruit.

This effect doesn't just shape memory; it drives attention, influence, and reputation. If you want to be unforgettable, be the anomaly, not the average. An early message to readers with my title, Market & Sell yourself, products, services like a Pineapple.

And yet, similarity matters too. In Gestalt Psychology, the *Similarity Principle* shows that our brain groups elements that share visual traits - color, shape, size - into unified wholes. When combined with *semantic networks,* this principle becomes a coaching tool I call: *Coaching with the Extreme Obvious.*

Speak from what's known - like a kids' book, a superhero, or a cultural icon - and use it to re-focus a deeper topic. It's non-confrontational persuasion. It lights up emotional closeness through what's already anchored in the mind. This is the *Ikea Effect:* we value what we've built ourselves. Emotional investment creates emotional relevance.

This chapter introduces the 15 Fundamental Anchors; emotional patterns and principles I've observed across cultures, timelines, and personal experiences. They are the roots of The Pineapple Theory.

Just as Earth has its four elements - Water, Fire, Wind, Soil - these anchors serve as emotional elements for human thriving. Insightfully, in reference to the 1997 movie The Fifth Element, we can harvest the perspective that everyone is a fifth element like being the key for life's *Law of Balance.* And, that Earth fundamental elements connect a person's past, present, and future for growth. Being the key is a timeless symbol referred as, The Key to Life.

Water
We are 60–70% water. It's life. It's flow. It's the reminder to keep our head above it.

Fire
Pineapples need tropical heat. Humans learn through flames, especially the ones we didn't expect, or from Hell.

Wind
Like a flag in the wind, sometimes we must trust the direction life gives us.

Soil
The foundation. The place we plant. The place we harvest. Even sandstorms can be seen through with emotional goggles.

Inspired by these elements, I asked: What if there were emotional anchors to help people manage their mind, body, and soul?

Like a pineapple plant, thriving requires roots. And in the *emotional illusions of life & time*, your true self is buried beneath cultural conditioning, other people's opinions, and childhood conclusions that became adult beliefs. If you don't pause in your temple - your mind - you will forget yourself. Chapter 3 speaks volume here.

With years of experience in Loss Prevention (LP) and global travel, I've observed emotional patterns across our *emotional timeline*, tens of thousands of years of trackable human behavior. I shared my conclusions in my book, *Worldwide Fruitful Travels with a Pineapple,* and here's a run-down of the anchors I detected:

- Classical conditioning, also known as Pavlov's conditioning.
- Darwin's theory.
- Law of Balance: Positive & Negative forces.
- Curiosity Gaps
- Need for fulfillment (purpose).

- Seek within – Emotional Batteries – Be Positive Curious.
- Egocentric theory & selfishness – Laziness – Belief.
- Cue words promoting reasoning rather than being trapped in the blur of the *emotional illusions with life & time.*
- Motive – Opportunity – Desire.
- Kindness – Truthful – Social & workplace etiquettes.
- Relief a pain – Save a fear – Support an ambition & hope.
- Love – Time – Health.
- Eat a full pineapple one bite at a time.
- Theoretical principle of 3.
- The *guinea pig* experiment

These anchors are not just ideas. They are emotional tools. They help you communicate better, regulate your emotions, and stay grounded when storms hit. They are the roots beneath the Crown.

So, grab your highlighter. Mark your pages. Because what follows is not just a list; it's a legacy. The 15 Fundamental Anchors of The Pineapple Theory are ready to be unearthed.

Classical conditioning

Humans holistic engineering with their thinking and feelings are wired from their own behaviors, cues, and influenced by their surroundings. Examples, and more about this topic with chapter, *Thriving Habits*.

- A boxer switches to beast mode once the bell of a round is heard.
- Wisely applied in the workplace, people completing a good deed expect a reward.
- How about your morning routine influencing if you will enjoy a good or bad day?

Darwin's theory

Darwin's theory of natural selection suggest that individuals of a species are more likely to survive in their environment and pass on their genes to the next generation when they inherit traits from their parents that are best suited for that specific environment. In this way, such traits become more widespread in the species and can lead eventually to the development of a new species.

Example: You become your surrounding because your surrounding is you. Or, how about the following perspective:

You start a new job with a new company, and it takes you from 3 to 6 months to adjust to your new environment. Also, your thinking and actions are from a *classical conditioning* of that same environment. Here's a deeper perspective about Darwin's theory.

From prior chapters, every person wears a mask. Not just one, but many, and switching between them depending on the situation, the people around them, and what they want to achieve. The face they show to the world is rarely their true self meaning it is a carefully constructed persona designed to fit into society, to be accepted, admired, or feared.

In psychology, it's referred to as, *the chameleon effect,* and it describes our tendency to unconsciously mimic the behaviors, gestures, and expressions of others. This mirroring phenomenon is thought to play a role in building rapport and strengthening social connections. Essentially, it suggests that we are naturally inclined to align our behavior with those we are interacting with, often without conscious awareness.

From childhood, people learn that showing their raw, unfiltered self is dangerous, also explaining why one show no one the truest reflection of who they really are. So, they adapt. They smile when they don't feel like it, they agree when they secretly disagree, they suppress their weaknesses and amplify their strengths. They craft identities that serve their interests like at work, in relationships, and even in solitude. Over time, these masks become second nature, blending so seamlessly with their personality that even they forget what lies beneath. They have lost themselves.

Per my books and serving this book's purpose, here's the paradox: The more masks a person wears, the less they know who they truly are. They become trapped in their own performance, uncertain whether their desires and beliefs are real or just another layer of the illusion they've created. And yet, they fear removing the mask because without it, they feel exposed, vulnerable, and lost. People do not interact with each other's true selves; they interact with each other's masks. And the one who understands this can shape their own mask to control how the world perceives them and in turn, how the world reacts to them.

London (UK) 2025, picture by Hozir Sahdat. Copyright: Steve "Mr. Pineapple" Mathieu

Law of Balance (LoB)

Trackable from the 14th century B.C, is the philosophy that life is positive & negative forces complementing each other when in balance. I suggest with my books that humans are that balance, with a *theoretical pineapple bridge* between their feelings & thinking, no matter if both forces are within or around.

London (UK) 2025, picture by Hozir Sahdat. Copyright: Steve "Mr. Pineapple" Mathieu

From a different angle and perspective with the patterns of our emotional timeline: For every positive creation, there will be the creation of its opposite. For every negative creation, humans are forced to create something positive. Or, where you win, there's a loss. And where there's a loss, there's win. Truly, we can't escape life's *Law of Balance.* Everything exists in duality, opposites, and these opposites are like two inseparable sides of the same coin yet. Let's dip a toe in water with the following example:

- Mouses have not created mouse traps.
- Bears have not created bear traps.
- But humans created the atomic bomb.

Or, how about the following thought-provoking challenges poking at people's inner warriors:

- Religions separate people when its purpose is to bring them together.
- Politics divide people where its purpose is to work for the people.
- Wealth classifies people always feeding tons of problems with society's non-supervised emotions.

- Race often becomes a surface judgment, disconnecting us from deeper understanding when we stop at appearances instead of being *positively curious* about the stories that shape each person's path.
- Lastly, each human enemy, the one that doesn't care about its human; Ego, and it took control of it all.

Let's start diving more into the LoB anchor with a deeper perspective.

Life/Death - Sun/Moon – Black/White - Hot/Cold – Summer/Winter - North/South – Positive/Negative – Wealth/Poverty – Success/Failures; the list about life's *Law of Balance* goes on. I suggest that it's fundamental to seek balance with our emotions & logic and insightfully with philosophy, which gives light to several Myths & Mythologies: Angle/Demon – Heart/Feather – Hulk – Werewolf – Batman's Two-Face – and so on. Here are pragmatic perspectives:

Life took form - or was created respectfully to your faith - with balance. As humans, we inherited these opposite traits because it's a natural environment that become us. In perspective, your brain is wired to divide the world into good and evil, us and them, right and wrong. But reality is never that simple yet, reality cannot escape because it always comes hunting when we do wrong, and when we choose to ignore it or barely glance at it. And when you do good, life still challenge you; even the last door on your path to peace is war.

Because it requires emotional energy already under pressure daily, the mind hates complexity, and it will always seek the least amount of emotional effort, an obvious exhibition of the masses complaining rather than acting as the solution, or simply following the masses without *positive curiosity*, nor being critical, referred to in psychology as, *social proof.*

Our mind craves clear answers even when they don't exist, that's why we divide the world into extremes; heroes and villains, truth and lies, winners and losers. A divided mind feels safer than a confused.

Look at politics, religion, social media or even sports. The more something is framed as a battle, the more engaged people become in the moment. We pick a side, we stop thinking, we just react. The more divided a group becomes, the easier it is. With this knowledge, the masses are easily manipulated by those who control the narrative, and they don't want unity.

Let's keep digging into more perspectives; if you feel chaos, thrive with the *Law of Balance* because it's growth, and it makes your pain worth something.

Introduce yourself to new ways of thinking, refreshing new ways to see & understand life because it's information for transformation leaving an old self behind. You see, experience is from what happened to one, like their failures, pains, and the brutal challenges of self-control. It takes hard days, sometimes stormy, for tomorrow's sunshine. But also, the sun is always above the clouds. The relationship with "the enemy" before its accepted as an "allied" is known as *Power Codex.*

Power Codex is not a recognized psychological term, but rather the title of books like *The Dark Psychology Codex*, which suggest using psychological tactics for influence and protection. These books, drawing from dark psychology, offer techniques for manipulation and control, and also provide guidance on recognizing and defending against them. They focus on concepts like *gaslighting* and emotional triggers to understand both the "darker side" of psychology and how to build personal defenses. The *Power Codex* concept can enable your way to overcome life's negative forces.

Alliance what the negative holding yourself back with bareness within the limits of what you already know will allow you to outgrow yourself. Balance is achieved like a pineapple farmer who is always *positively curious* to nurture fresh & modern cultivation methods to grow the freshest & most juicy pineapples. Without action, there isn't any progress because pineapples don't grow from magic beans. The *Law of Balance* is an anchor and cue to thrive with your emotional management:

- Feeling Angry, sing to feel better.
- Feeling Anxious, pause & breathe.
- Feeling Stressed, exercise.
- Feeling Sad, have you had gratitude?
- Feeling Impatient? Have you reflected on progress?

How about nurturing your mindset for balance:
- What if discomfort is growth?
- What if problems are in fact, challenges?
- What if rejection was redirection?
- What if darkness reveals light?
- What if failures were in fact, lessons?
- What if fear was a task and a teacher?

What if it's your cue for emotional balance with action?
- If you miss somebody, have you called?
- If you want to be understood, have you explained?
- If bothered by a question, have you asked?
- If you don't like something, how about fixing it?
- If you want something, have you worked for it?

What if it's your cue to become appreciative?
- When there's sadness, you get to know happiness.
- When there's noise, you appreciate silence.
- When there's absence, you appreciate presence.
- We learn tolerance from intolerance.
- We learn kindness from the unkind.

Or, what if it's your cue to acknowledge, be humble with, and value your blessings?

- Your terrible job is the dream of the unemployed.
- Your house is the dream of the homeless.
- Your smile is the dream of depression.
- Your health is the dream of the ill.
- What you think is negative in your life might just be someone else dream life.

LoB is also a cue to better interact & understand others, yourself, or both. In fact, the quality of your life is deeply connected to the relationships you build. Studies show that 85% of your happiness comes from the people you surround yourself with; friends, family, mentors, and even the communities you engage in. It's *Darwin Theory* in motion.

In perspective, if it feels dark within, hang where it's enlightening which is a powerful philosophy from several Myths & Mythologies when people are feeling lost in their life. Let's reflect for a moment about the following wise perspective. Sadly, but also a deep inspiration for this book, living is to suffer. Many people feel lost when they experience pain, and their pain feels like darkness. It's often them seeking a means to survive with the attempt to find some meaning in their suffering. From this profound knowledge about humans, several Biblical figures are drawn with light surrounding their head to visualize an enlighten mind, then follows both open harms to welcome you, and it is framed with the following statement speaking volume about the LoB as a cue to offer a solution when a person self-acknowledged their heart feels dark: *"[Name of the Myth or Mythology's all mighty] experienced them all. What you feel, once was felt. It knows the way."*

A genuine challenge though about the *Law of Balance* is finding people who will recognize your success as if it was theirs and here's why.

You don't want your friends to succeed, you want them to do well, just never better than you. Every time someone close to you rises, parts of you hopes they will fall. I know it sounds rough and thought-provocative because rarely will someone admit it. But deep down, their success feels like your failure. When someone else rises, you feel like you're falling. It's irrational but it's deeply wired into human nature. Referred to in psychology as *zero-sum bias*, it suggests a tendency to perceive situations as *zero-sum* games, where one person's gain inevitably means another's loss, even when cooperation and mutual benefit are possible. One word sums it all: Envy.

Lastly, about this motion of thoughts, everything you hate in others reflects your own shortcomings. You'll despise arrogance because deep down you crave that same confidence. You'll judge selfishness because you wish you had the courage to put yourself first. You'll mock weakness because it reminds you of your own fears. The *Law of Balance* can be projection, a mirror of truth about yourself, and it's a coding about human nature. Projection is a psychological defense mechanism for which, instead of admitting your flaws, you will assign them to others. Examples:

- The weak will call the world unjust.
- The envious call ambition greed.
- The unfaithful become obsessed with loyalty, every insult, every criticism, every judgement.

It's not about the other person, it's a glimpse into the speaker's soul, and if you actively listen to what people – and yourself – condemn, you will see their deepest wounds with the purpose to provide balance.

The curiosity gap

A *curiosity gap* is the empty space between what you know and do not know. Everyone experiences a *curiosity gap*, although they will say otherwise, their behavior never lies meaning that limited truly knows how to manage their emotions with it, and it is the trigger of several emotional conflicts within & around. Its people's own trickery by their emotional illusions with *life & time*. From our history, here's an example about the *curiosity gap* inspired from my travel to London in March 2022, when I admired Stonehenge.

London (UK) 2022, picture & copyright by Steve "Mr. Pineapple" Mathieu

Stonehenge; a prehistoric monument on Salisbury Plain in Wiltshire, England. It consists of an outer ring of vertical sarsen standing stones, each around 13 feet high, seven feet wide, and weighing around 25 tons, topped by connecting horizontal lintel stones.

When not written, history can't be entirely confirmed. And without facts, theory becomes, and Stonehenge was:

- Checkpoint for Aliens.

- Burial site.
- Tables for Giants.
- Ceremonial site.
- Teleportation portal.
- A Memorial as one's gift to another.
- A Lego set for a Giant baby.
- The very first Hard Rock Café!

The above is what many think used to be with what is now called Stonehenge and owned by the Crown. From several patterns with history, with previous eras of humans' timeline, I personally think Stonehenge was a strategic calendar place to read the patterns of astronomy.

At the conclusion of my research, and they are a fundamental anchor, I suggest that the following combination of words: "I think" – "I assume" – "I guess" are cues to activate one's *positive curiosity.*

Until humans discover any form of writing or drawing explaining what Stonehenge *was*, it will remain what humans think Stonehenge *is.* What we think requires keeping our mind agile and open to accept what will once become, a fact by accepting it. Philosophically per my theory, *what was still is.* From a Prehistoric era to now, the following principle – more about it later with this book - is proof of concept:

Master File
Journal
Communicate

Several eras drew what they did or witnessed. Several eras engraved symbols about what they witnessed and how they lived. Drawings and symbols have patterns to be decoded by our current era of the timeline. All followed the *Master File – Journal – Communicate* principle.

The *Master File – Journal – Communicate* principle is valuable for today's era. No matter if applied in the workplace or in a personal diary, it is a powerful tool to decode patterns, observe opportunities, self-reflect with our own writings, or assist our memory like what to purchase at the grocery store.

Ones' pineapple inner sweetness can positively breath inside/out when one is *positively curious* with what they think they know – is – should and could.

Ones' pineapple shell will serve as a filter to accept what are facts without being trapped in the emotional illusion and blur of their imagination, and the emotional illusion of their surroundings which is nicely presented to viewers with the 2022 movie, Wakanda Forever. It's uncovered that Vibranium can be found elsewhere, one of the Crown's guards said: *"I still can't believe that Vibranium can be found outside of Wakanda. This changes everything that we know. The Great Mound, all of the Legends and Fables. Those stories are seared in my mind."*

Let's add a serving of psychology about the *curiosity gap.* I refer to humans' emotions as an *emotional illusion life & time* because in part, manipulative people will leverage the *curiosity gap* to manipulate someone's mind and the trick doesn't lie in the words a person speak, it lies in the words a person don't speak in the gaps, and the mind is left to fill these gaps that were created. When essential information is missing, or when inconsistent information is presented, it causes the brain to unconsciously fill in those gaps. It does so with the guidance of the subtle hints a person provided leading someone to the conclusion, meaning there's a reach without them even realizing it. This works so brutally because it exploits – not limited to - three psychological concepts as follows.

The power of curiosity, which suggests a drive to seek knowledge and experience, leading to increased learning, creativity, and overall well-being, as well as being associated with intelligence and problem-solving abilities

Priming, which suggests that exposure to one stimulus (the prime) can influence a person's response to a subsequent stimulus (the target), often without conscious awareness, by activating related mental representations or associations.

The *availability heuristic,* which suggests that people tend to judge the likelihood or frequency of events based on how easily examples of those events come to mind, leading to potential biases in decision making.

Need for fulfillment

Bareness is madness, meaning that a bored human will become negativity in life. Humans must live to fulfill a purpose, no matter its size and duration. They must always have at least one ongoing. Allow me to deep dive with the following perspective.

Truth be told, you were never asked to be born and yet, here you are on a planet with 8 billion people. What if pineaHapply thriving at cultivating your seed for greatness could serve to enjoy a more joyful, fulfilling, and peaceful living?

Another truth must be told; it's not that easy. The good news is that when facing several challenges, your mind becomes stronger, like what is a stronger body from continuous hard labor.

Living with ourselves can easily become challenging from time to time, even if many refuse to admit it to themselves, and we must add 8 billion people with the same challenge along with the attempt of living respectfully together without knowing each other. Sadly, even when people do know each other, there isn't much peace. Through my careful observation with several patterns of our emotional timeline, I suggest that respect, social etiquette, and kindness substitute the absence of love.

So much happiness depends on how we choose to look at the World, and ourselves. Cultivating your seed for greatness must start with a purpose, the *why*, becoming the thing that wakes you up in the morning. Then you'll thrive but bear in mind that you will not live your life with a single purpose, meaning that you must have one purpose after the other, no matter what size they are. Speaking of my *theoretical 3 principle* fundamental anchor, I suggest the following categorization:

- Short term, meaning small accomplishments or quick wins.
- Medium term, often from 3 to 12 months.
- Long term, often refers to those big questions, for example: *"Where do you see yourself 5 years from now?"* How about the long term & life purpose inspired by several Myths & Mythologies, meaning the purpose of serving and continuing the path built by their all mighty?

My mentorship tip is always having one ongoing purpose for each category. They become goals for yourself, something to work on, future achievements becoming lessons learned from your experiences. Each path for each purpose will have obstacles, and each obstacle is your truest path. You will learn, build, and cultivate yourself from your experience with the obstacle course. Your path is your thriving greatness.

Moving yourself and others with persuasion always starts with a *why*, speaking of a purpose. I speak of this along with examples in my book, *Worldwide fruitful travels with a pineapple,* and following your reading of this book, listen actively to yourself and others, and you will hear many people starting with their *how* instead of their *why*. When this happens, it's a cue for *positive curiosity*. Another mentorship tip to cultivate greatness is as follows:

If one speaks their *how* first, seek within and *be positively curious*, ask them about their *why*. Suddenly, you will feel their *why* becoming a reason to live and bear almost any *how,* meaning that their *how* becomes much more engaging & influential. In fact, people look more attractive and fruitful when they speak about the things they truly are passionate about, and their passion is from their ambitious emotional investment about the *why* they can accomplish what others are not hungry enough for.

Here's a generic example when it starts with a *why* extracted for a speech, I made to a group of entrepreneurs, in February 2024:

"Since October 2020, every day I wake up with the excitement and passion about the following philosophical purpose:

"Theoretically, what if adding a pineapple to people's life, leadership, and business recipes could assist living more "pineHapply", together?

Working backwards, for several years, waking up was simply to get another day done. "Working for the man" as we may say.

When COVID impacted the world, forced to stay home as a mitigation measure for everyone's safety until a cure to neutralize the roots was made available, a large portion of society in several countries demonstrated what happens to humans when they are bored. They think, act, and speak with madness. More than that, managing themselves so no one else pays the emotional price is lacking.

This is way beyond COVID, it's experienced since more than 10,000 years of trackable history. You see, we are teaching history, but we don't learn from it. The wises spoke, even in today's era and yet, no one truly listens.

With our current era of the timeline, the more technology evolves, the more humans thinking moves backwards. Technology must evolve but it should not undo humans' ability to think.

Humans are an interesting species not capable of truly accepting how they are, and when society negatively thinks, acts, and speaks without owning it because they seek around instead of within, it is life giving everyone lemons.

The classic proverbial phrase that when life gives you lemons, make lemonade, I don't buy it. You see, what are you truly fixing out of lemonade, it is still negativity, simply presented differently. It's challenging to fix a problem with what the problem is. It becomes an escalation of the problem.

So, it was COVID, for myself and others, I started to wake up to fulfill a purpose requiring passion, something making it exciting to wake up for. Yes, I sold my lemons and purchased a pineapple. (…)"

In life, one without a purpose to fulfill is bored, and bareness triggers negativity with their thinking, speaking, and actions. That's only true if you come to the self-realization that your fulfilment of a purpose is not for you, it must be for the positive impact towards others, and that becomes your fulfillment to harvest more happiness. Add a pineapple to the recipe, and it's more "pineHapply" living.

Always live your life fulfilling purposes because when you have purposes, you are passionate about giving something to others and it should be something good and useful. To support you at making the right choice for each purpose, here's a suggested self-reflective filter:

- Is it free of all forms of Hate?
- Is it free of Division?
- Is it free of all forms of Harm?
- Is it compliant with the books of rules?
- Is it inspired from what facts are, meaning free of what could emotionally trick you such as: What you think is, should, could, assume, and not source from gossip?

To move the world, you must first move yourself. Having purposes in your life is more meaningful when you are always looking to grow and working toward a goal. Cultivating your seed for greatness with purposes will inspire a blossom of ambitions, and your motivation must be compelling to overcome the obstacles in your way because there will be obstacles.

In life, there is no greater thing you can do with your life and your work than follow your passions because that serves the world and you. Meaning that, your process to cultivate greatness will likely start by asking yourself what you would be or do and then, you must do what you must do.

The beginning is the most important part of the journey, meaning that your journey of a thousand steps must start with one first definite step forward. Like your first step as a child, you started with one along with a few falls, you rise and look at you go now!

You already have a seed for greatness within; you were born with it. It's inherited. What if your next step could be to give yourself the purpose of always learning how to cultivate your seed to harvest a blooming and thriving greatness?

Ikigai, referred to in Japanese as a reason for being, the thing that gets up in the morning.

Seek within

Seek within is one of the three-core fundamentals of my theory because everything starts with you. Seek within for the following reasons:

When self-acknowledge and as a habit, you easily with noblest move yourself in life by improving yourself, not by crushing others.

When self-acknowledge and as a habit, you will realize that the more you value things outside your control, the less control you will have. From a different perspective, when you seek within, you have power over your mind and not outside events, and that's a strength within you.

When self-acknowledge and as a habit, you will realize that suffering arises from trying to control what is uncontrollable, or from neglecting what is within your power.

When self-acknowledge and as a habit, you realize that the attempt to seek the good in external things is a waste of your emotional energy – for example, comparison being the thieve of your happiness - you realize you must seek them in yourself.

When all listed principles & concepts from The Pineapple Theory are wisely observed, you realize that people will do anything, no matter how mind blowing, to avoid facing their own soul. Meaning that, many people lack curiosity with their emotions, and they don't have the care nor courage to look at life beneath the surface. It's all about whatever shines on the tip of the iceberg. In other words, people have excuses for everything, becoming their roadblock for growth.

When self-acknowledge and as a habit, you realize that when you seek within, your vision becomes clearer because you are looking into your own heart. Meaning that, if you seek around, you dream, but if you seek within, you awake.

Lastly, when self-acknowledge and as a habit, you realize that there's no possibility of real peace when the ignorance of your ego is your master. When you seek within, you make peace and realize that mistakes are always forgivable, if you have the courage to admit them, and when they don't repeat.

Emotional Batteries

The *emotional batteries* are the second of the three-core fundamentals of my theory because we are made of energy, we have emotions, and I merged both then called them *emotional batteries.*

In fact, a typical person at rest produces around 100 watts of energy, roughly equivalent to the power of a standard light bulb. During strenuous activity, this can increase significantly, reaching 300-400 watts for sustained periods or even over 2000 watts in short bursts like sprinting.

It's no wonder why movie writers are energized to humans' energy, like the 1999 movie The Matrix, suggesting that humans are batteries for the machine, or Marvel's Studios 2021 Eternals, suggesting that a large amount of living humans produces enough energy for a new celestial to burst through its egg, meaning a planet.

Thriving at cultivating your greatness, more peace, love, and freedom requires cultivating positivity within to harvest positivity around, and you must *seek within* to assess the level of energy of your emotional batteries. Meaning yes, thriving at being great & conquering yourself from your inner wars is exhausting, and you must cultivate the habit of recharging them. I could speak an entire Ted Talk about the *emotional batteries.* High-level, here's are refreshing perspectives, three recharging processes I suggest adding to your life recipe.

The *daily feel good* and/or the *daily emotional booster,* is that one thing you must do daily making you feel good and recharge. For me, it's weightlifting, and I plan it before anything else even if I must wake up at 3h00AM.

The *quarterly booster* is a once a quarter planned 3 or 4-day weekend feeling like a vacation booster, meaning you organize it like a vacation. Plus, it fulfils a short-term purpose.

Lastly, the *annual booster,* meaning within a year, is at least one full week of non-interrupted vacation. It is also considered a purpose, like a medium size project if you choose to travel overseas. And I strongly recommend travelling because travelling is not a reward for working, it is education for living.

Be positively curious

The concept of being *positively curious* is the last and third core fundamental of my theory, and the most impactful.

You can only *seek within* and assess your *emotional batteries* if you are *positively curious.* But there are countless reasons for this valuable concept with the purpose of cultivating the most blooming seed for greatness within you and conquering your inner battles.

You must *be positively curious* to self-acknowledge and cultivate a habit of excellence about all listed principles & concepts from this book. Remember the *curiosity gap*, how about closing the gap with your *positive curiosity*?

Being *positively curious* suggests becoming curious with positive emotions as a very first step because positivity within is reflected around. It's the *Ideomotor Theory* in motion. It's *Predictive Processing Theory* to achieve a positive outcome.

People tricked by their *curiosity gap* with the emotional illusions with *life & time* discuss people, and others will discuss events. When *positively curious*, applying all the principles & concepts of my books, you discuss ideas.

If you *seek within* by appearing, content, and sounding foolish with positive energy and *positive curiosity*, you're not keeping peace by force, you are achieving peace because you understand, and understanding is the root of everything blooming in life.

Your *positive curiosity* can become an awesome bonding with others. Everyone has their story. If you meet someone with a kind heart, be *positively curious* because they likely felt the most pain. *Be positively curious* about their story and be inspired, it becomes valuable surrounding.

Imagine meeting someone who takes time to truly know you. Someone who listens - not to judge or correct - but to understand. Your past. Your experiences. Your perspectives. They ask with care. They speak with respect. They act with authenticity. Now imagine: What if you could be that person?

As generational cycles accelerate through technology, we must not let speed undo our ability to think. We must not let convenience replace connection. Because in life, most people assume others are fine, but they're only glancing at the surface. In truth, many are living their hardest moments alone. Not because they want to, but because no one noticed the cues. No one activated their *positive curiosity*. Unless you're *positively curious,* you won't know:

The silent struggles someone carries.
The project quietly fueling their ambition.
The mindset shaping their day.
The feedback they're afraid to share.

The same applies with people speaking as if everything is perfect. When this happens,

I'm always at the top of my *positive curiosity* because often, they have the worst demons within. They feed their *Shadow Self* without realizing it anymore. The same applies with the silent ones. The *Law of Balance* is once more experienced.

Not limited to, but lastly, you embody greatness, more peace, love, and freedom when *positively curious* with one's advice. Their advice can cultivate improvement with how you think, act, and speak to harvest more greatness in your life, and the World. Their advice are seeds for thought.

When you cultivate *positive curiosity*, you harvest a clearer understanding, then you pineHapply thrive. Your *positive curiosity* allowed establishing a connection given the welcoming value of a pineapple for empathy and train your inner warrior at being self-aware with empathy and here's why: Victim often becomes manipulators, meaning that empathy without awareness becomes self-destruction. Never hurt others to heel yourself – Never hurt yourself to heal others.

***Egocentric theory* & selfishness – Laziness – Belief**
The Emotional Illusion of "Everyone Thinks Like Me"

First introduced in *Feel & Think Like a Pineapple*, I shared that when lived blindly, in extremes, and without balance - whether positive or negative - *egocentric theory*, laziness, and belief are the topmost triggers for human conflict on our wicked planet. In fact, they are emotional triggers behind human conflict and growth.

But here's the twist: these same triggers, when understood and used with kindness and emotional clarity, become tools for positive persuasion. Like an artist with a kind heart, you can sculpt them into emotional wisdom.

Let's explore each one.

Egocentric theory & selfishness
Life is a pattern. A cycle. From the birth of a star to its supernova. From the millions of shining stars in the universe can be found the Milky Way, and the second rock from its star; Eart. And on this peculiar planet, humans are both the problem and the solution.

As humans, we are emotional creatures. Life is simple but humans make it difficult. And when our emotions dominate our thinking, we become dangerous to ourselves, and others. Like pigeons locked onto a goal, we lose peripheral vision. We react, not reflect. We justify poor behavior with urgency, like being late to work becomes a license to mistreat others.

This is *egocentric theory* in action.

Jean Piaget first described it in children: the belief that everyone sees the world as they do. "Everyone thinks like me." But adults carry this too. It's a variant of *Projection Bias*; assuming others share your values, logic, and emotional priorities.

When they don't, we feel disappointed. But disappointment isn't caused by what people do, it's caused by what we expected them to do. That gap between reality and projection is what hurts. Psychologically, it's called *Expectation Violation*, and it's amplified by the *Default Mode Network* (DMN), which attaches self-referential meaning to external events.

To break this cycle, we need *cognitive reframing*. Ask yourself: Did they violate a commitment? Or did I expect them to follow rules they never agreed to?

This shift activates the prefrontal cortex, regulating the emotional surge and restoring perspective. You begin to see people as they are; not as you hoped they'd be.

We all have an inner child. And unless we evolve past the preoperational phase, we remain emotionally blind. The word *believe* is a cue: it often means "I don't truly know." Without curiosity, belief becomes a trap.

Self-awareness is key, especially in leadership. You can't expect others to think, act, or speak like you just because you're ready. Understand the world as it is, not as you wish it to be.

Selfishness is the adult version of egocentrism. And we all have it. The question is: do we balance it?

COVID-19's toilet paper chaos was a circus of selfishness. Loyalty often follows need, not values. And when needs change, so does loyalty. But applied positively, selfishness becomes self-care. Let every situation be what it is - not what you think it should be - and you may find the key to happiness.

History repeats itself. On 27 July 2023, a country halted rice exports. Grocery store chaos followed. Humans didn't learn from history, they reenacted it.

And when ego is insulted, negativity erupts. Compliment the identity but critique the action. That's emotional wisdom. As Goethe said: *"You can easily judge the character of a man by how he treats those who can do nothing for him."*

In life, remember the following: Disrespect will close doors that apologies can't open. Be careful how you treat people you think you don't need.

Beliefs- *The Placebo, the Prison, and the Pathway*
Emotions are the first fence. Thinking is the second. When they work together in balance, wisdom reigns.

But many act without thinking. They live impulsively, like selfish kings. And without tools to train the emotional muscle, they remain stuck. Sadly, most schools don't teach self-confidence, passion, or love.

Throughout Earth's timeline, Myths and Mythologies offered emotional guidance.

They taught us to befriend our inner voice. Because in life, you speak to yourself more than anyone else. Your thoughts shape your reality. One bad thought can ruin your day. One good thought can change your life. You are your own cure. Your thoughts are your medicine. Your mind believes what you tell it. So, tell it something kind.

The amygdala - your almond-shaped fear center - can hijack your confidence with negative perfection. Like Spider-Man's *spidy sense*, it warns of danger. But it also feeds illusions. "You can't do it." "You'll fail." "You're not enough." Negative self-talk is self-sabotage.

But courage is your inner warrior's ability to face the unknown. Studies show that anxiety increases blood flow to the amygdala. Confidence shifts it to the cerebral cortex, where logic lives.

Beliefs are powerful. They're placebos. They soothe, guide, and sometimes blind. But when beliefs cause pain, challenge them. They may be lying to you. And lies hate to be challenged. Truth invites discomfort, then healing. When a person's voice lies, and then speaks the truth, no one believes them. When an intelligent one knows the truth and claims it's a lie, they are a criminal.

Beliefs can make you feel pain, fear, stress, anxiety about what you cannot control in life, and it's a waste of your emotional energy. Reframe with the Law of Balance, seek within because you can control your inside:

What if you could turn a disadvantage into an advantage?
What if you could turn a liability into an asset?
What if a failure could become a success, and your defeat into victory?

You don't need to force someone to believe something. You don't need to argue, convince, or debate. You just need to be the first thought, the first idea, the first suggestion because once a seed is planted, the mind bends reality to nurture it without ever questioning where it came from.

Referred to as *cognitive anchoring,* it's a psychological bias that describes how people rely too heavily on the first piece of information they receive. This information is called the *anchor*. Anchoring can lead to poor decisions in many situations, such as when buying a car, negotiating salaries, or making medical diagnoses.

The first piece of information someone receives about a topic becomes their reference point shaping how they interpret everything after. If you meet someone and hear they are difficult to work with, your brain looks for proof even if they're perfectly fine. The media is an *extreme obvious* about *cognitive anchoring* into society's mind, and when a country leader imposes a selection of media only because they release what they want society to hear from them, it's a serious threat. My mom doesn't realize it, but she's a real sucker with this because her voice is not hers about a topic, but the one she heard from the media being her single anchor point.

If someone tells you a restaurant is overrated, your brain notices the flaws first, even if the food is amazing. If a politician is labeled a threat, or a savior, every action they take gets filtered through that lens. Logic doesn't even matter anymore.

This psychology is highly valuable with the purpose at breaking through your own self-beliefs from your own thoughts, and if someone anchored information about what you do not know, nor have you experienced it like a *guinea pig, be positively curious.* But you also can thrive by planting a thought in someone's mind without them realizing. Here are three proposed steps:

1. Be first, introduce the idea before anyone else does.
2. Wrap it in a question or casual remark so it feels organic.
3. Let them reach the conclusion themselves because once they believed it was their own thought, it's locked in.

Here's a pragmatic approach with the purpose of winning over a person's deep belief. Humans' ego is so huge that their brain automatically blocks anything that doesn't align with their existing beliefs, no matter how good the idea is. When a person contradicts someone else, any objective discussion is dead, but people don't resist their own thoughts. The trick to implant an idea is to align it with their existing belief and then add a little detail that shifts their entire perspective.

In psychology, it's referred to as the *addition trick*, and it suggests *cognitive biases*, mental shortcuts, and the human tendency to simplify complex tasks and it works because of the following reference in psychology, called *cognitive consistency*, suggesting that humans have an innate drive to maintain internal harmony and coherence in their thoughts, beliefs, and behaviors, seeking to reduce discomfort when inconsistencies arise.

Cognitive consistency theory was developed by Leon Festinger in 1957, stating that when individuals are confronted with new information that conflicts with their existing beliefs, they experience psychological discomfort. To alleviate this discomfort, the brain either changes the belief or rejects the new information. However, this resistance is reduced when the new information is small or seemingly insignificant referred to in psychology as *just noticeable difference*, and it refers to the smallest detectable difference in a stimulus that a person can reliably distinguish 50% of the time.

This is where the *addition trick* comes in. Instead of directly challenging someone's belief, you introduce a subtle addition that slightly shifts their worldview. Since this addition doesn't cause major dissonance, the person accepts it as part of their existing framework. Over time, this minor adjustment can lead to a larger change in their overall perspective. Personally, I have always valued a good question with the purpose to challenge my self-created belief, or assumption, and the *addition trick* speaks volume about the *butterfly effect.*

This process of *cognitive consistency theory* is reinforced by *priming* someone's brain with a small, related detail, because you set the stage for them to accept the shift more easily. In psychology, it's *framing,* and it also plays a role here because it suggests that how information is presented, or framed, significantly influences how people perceive, evaluate, and make decisions, even if the underlying information remains the same. Meaning that by presenting this small addition in a way that aligns with the person's current worldview, you reduce the likelihood of resistance. The brain is more likely to integrate information that feels congruent with what it already believes, even if the new idea is subtly different.

I often remind; What if it's not about the belief one follows – rather – what if it's about how one chooses to live with their beliefs?

So don't argue. Don't be convinced. Plant the seed. Let the mind bend reality to nurture it because a mastery about being *positively curious* is when you are capable to understand a thought different from yours without having to accept it.

Jim Carrey
Cheers to all the people who can change their minds when presented with information that contradicts their belief.

Laziness - *The Easy Road That Leads Nowhere*

Humans are wired for efficiency. Laziness is natural. It worsens with a low level of *emotional energy*. But when emotions dominate and curiosity fades, laziness becomes resistance.

Technology fuels this. "Why spend energy when tech made it easy?" But growth requires effort. The more you train the emotional muscle, the stronger it gets.

In psychology, *Indolence* describes laziness: the unwillingness to act despite ability. *Social Proof* explains why we follow the crowd. Ratings, reviews, influencers; they shape behavior.

Most people won't change until pain forces them. When there's urgency activated by the amygdala survival mode. When tired of pain being their teacher. They are reactive, not proactive. They wait until their roots touch hell before seeking light.

"Out of sight, out of mind." If it's not close, it's not cared for. Fear creates proximity. It becomes a mental picture. And when framed correctly, it motivates change. Psychological concepts such as *Loss aversion, social proof,* the *authority principle* -or the media, social media, and more are leveraged to give fear proximity, and pain similarity to as many people as possible.

The Pineapple Theory reminds us: *What was, still is.* History teaches. But humans rarely learn. Then our timeline repeats itself with succeeding infinite loopholes. We touch the fire to confirm it burns. We love comfort zones even when they lead nowhere.

Laziness joins ego and belief in resisting change. Unless accepted from within, people resist what they're told. They speak before they think. They react before they reflect.

People with knowledge speak when necessary. People without it speak often.

Final Reflection

Egocentric theory, belief, and laziness are not flaws. They are emotional patterns. When lived blindly, they trigger conflict. But when understood, they become tools for growth.

This anchor invites you to self-assess, reflect, and recharge. To challenge your illusions. To balance your ego. To plant beliefs that heal. And to choose effort over ease.

Because thriving isn't about perfection. It's about presence. And the pineapple stands tall, not because it's flawless, but because it's deeply rooted.

Cue words for reasoning

I suggest that you cultivate greatness and prevent war within if you become *positively curious* following your active listening with yourself, and others, with the following cue words:

- What you and others ***think is, should, and could*** is not a fact. *Be positively curious.*
- What you and others ***assume, guess, predict*** is not a fact. *Be positively curious.*
- When you and others say ***because, if, and buts,*** they are often roadblocks of self-awareness, they disguise a close mind, and they are excuses and not a search for positive solutions leading to results. *Be positively curious.*

Motive – Opportunity – Desire

They must be answered when completing an investigation, and no matter if positive or negative, people's thoughts, actions, and voice always origin from a Motive – Opportunity – and Desire.

Kindness – Truthful – Social & workplace etiquettes

Shared as a philosophy throughout The Pineapple Theory and my *guinea pig* experiences, this anchor begins with a simple truth:

When you are kind and truthful, life is much more fruitful.

It's a small sentence, easy to carry in your mind, and it's a thriving, blooming, and valuable currency for your life. To truly thrive nd win, train your inner strength not to fear failure, rejection, loss, or disrespect; but always, above all, remain kind, respectful, and well-mannered.

Love all. Trust a few. Never – ever - harm.

In today's world, money, followers, and titles impress. But kindness, calmness, and good manners are often ignored. Conquer and thrive with respect, for yourself, and others. And observe the following five environments, where poor behavior often reveals itself:

(5) Driving
(4) 24/7 Gyms
(3) Public Toilets
(2) Retail Stores
(1) When they think no one is watching

With open eyes and an open mind, work through your roadblocks instead of using them as excuses. For tens of thousands of years, myths and mythologies have reminded us: *an eye is always watching.*

Etiquette and manners are the glue of society, like clusters of flowers forming a sweet pineapple. Another philosophy from The Pineapple Theory:

It starts with you, because it's not about you.

Etiquette and manners

Everyone has the freedom to act with kindness, respect, and good manners. They currency of character in a World of emotional illusions. What you plant, you harvest. And when love is absent, its substitutes are respect, kindness, and etiquette. Trust is the ultimate element; never breach it, with yourself or others.

In Japan, this philosophy is lived. Children don't take exams until age 10. Instead, they learn manners first, respect for people, animals, nature, and teamwork. They clean their classrooms, corridors, and toilets. They learn to value their environment because they've invested in it. This is the *Ikea Effect:* we value what we help create.

Tokyo, a city of over 125 million, is clean despite having almost no public trash bins. Why? Because people respect each other. Even smoking is regulated with designated areas, no second-hand smoke, no stray cigarette burns.

Copyright Steve "Mr. Pineapple" Mathieu – Tokyo (JP) 2023

Meanwhile, in Montreal, spring reveals the trash buried under winter snow. Summer campers leave behind litter in small towns. Society blames everything except itself. But the solution isn't more bins or policing, it's cultural. It's human.

A baseball experiment showed this contrast. After a Japan–USA game, the Japanese side was spotless. The American side? Rubbish everywhere. One side respected the space. The other relied on staff. The difference? Culture. Ownership.

<u>Kindness</u>

Every time you choose not to do good, you become guilty of that choice. We all owe someone. We all benefit by helping others.

Do not do to others what angers you if done to you by others.

Don't make others pay the emotional price for your unmanaged emotions. Everyone you meet is fighting an inner battle. If you can help, help. If you can't, don't harm. Be kind whenever possible—because it's always possible.

Kindness generates a good attitude, a good heart, and happiness—for you and others. But many are kind only to those they want to impress. Loyalty often follows need, not values. When needs change, so does loyalty. Accepting this is a conquered battle within.

In the workplace, this pattern is clear. People are polite to upper management, but fake to others. I recall a Store Manager who dropped our conversation mid-sentence to greet a VP like a teenage girl meeting her crush. It was pathetic. Worse, the VP welcomed it—flattered by fake behavior. This nurtures a culture of disrespect.

Honest people are kind to everyone—not just those with titles. But they often feel alone. Still, kindness never loses value. Disrespect closes doors that apologies can't reopen.

Be careful how you treat people you think you don't need.

My title, Market & Sell yourself, products, services like a pineapple reminds us that people will always remember how you made them feel. Your actions are the mirror of your character. With 8 billion humans on Earth, each person who remembers your kindness can change the world.
In the book, inspired by Joe Girard's 1:250 rule: one client likely knows or influences 250 others. Multiply that by the 10,000 people you'll meet in your lifetime. Retail, travel, hospitality, every "hello" matters.

I used to greet people with, "How can I contribute to keeping your day joyful?" Most smiled. Some didn't. One even said, *"Don't talk to me and I'll have a good day."* That's the 1%; outside the common-sense standard deviation.

But even a shy smile back is a win. Many aren't used to receiving kindness. Some are disturbed by your peace. Others are troubled by your smile; it confronts their inner demons.

You're not smiling because you're happy. You're happy because you're smiling. Kindness pollinates. One person remembering your greatness can ripple outward. Never underestimate your contribution.

Ichi-go ichie
Japanese meaning: Treasure every encounter, for it will never recur.

Love – Time – Health, and Relief a pain – Save a fear – Support an ambition & hope.

Introduced with my book, *Market & Sell yourself, products, services like a pineapple,* is an important mindset when self-reflecting with the purpose of earning a person's heart. Extracted from the book:

"This mindset is valuable for yourself, and others. In life, no matter if it's from your own thoughts or from others, if something does not provide you with at least one of the 3, move on. In your position, how you will choose to think/act/speak must give Love – Time – Health and, it is often bridged

with the following three: Relief a pain – Save a fear – realistically cultivate their ambitions & hopes.

I must share, you may find the following manipulative, but understanding humans' emotions better, their psychology, and how to bridge it with rationality is a powerful combination in sales, when leading a team in the workplace, and within society. When helping others by providing Love – Time – Health, you are putting them first, and you are demonstrating respect and concern for their needs and desires. Your communication will be impactful, persuasive, and will reach people's emotions. When becoming agile with this tool, it becomes an enhance ability, it is you providing positive energy, positive thoughts, and positive solutions. When people are positively moved, they purchase. What you understand and can use better than the average requires to be from a place of good like a pineapple farmer. That's an important responsibility, it cultivates emotions within others, and those emotions will be remembered. Those emotions will be given back to you."

Eat a full pineapple one bite at a time

Pineapples don't grow from magic beans and neither do you. Like eating a full pineapple, in life, move yourself one small, sweet pineapple bite at a time. Similarly with history to educate people, several cultures have spoken such a message:

African proverb
"The best way to eat an elephant in your path is to cut him up into little pieces." Meaning, the best way to solve a problem is to tackle it bit by bit, one step at a time.

Chinese proverb
"You can't get fat with one mouthful." Meaning, if you want something, be patient and persevere because good things take time, things aren't accomplished right away.

English
"Biting more than you can chew." Meaning, don't take on more responsibilities than you're able to handle. Also serving as an idiom, meaning you're trying to accomplish something that is too difficult for you.

Japanese culture
Kaizen, meaning a method for transforming habits incrementally, one step at a time, in order to continuously improve.

The Pineapple Theory
Like an ananas growing millimeters at the time, focus on the steps in front of you, not the whole staircase.

Theoretical principle of 3

First introduced with my unlisted title – Theoretically the Origin of The Pineapple Theory - I suggest that all great things come in 3. Let's dive deep into several perspectives before we soon move on to the next chapter building on this one.

I don't do, follow, or live by numerology. Although, I have observed an important pattern with our emotional timeline with *life & time,* and there is one number I strongly value & recommend applying with the purpose to thrive with your decision making and persuasion that speaks strongly. When we take quality time to pause and carefully observe, it surrounds us nearly all the time. That number is: Three (3).

The number 3 was and still held a powerful symbolism. Think about good things coming in 3s, I call it *3-pack,* that are frequently represented from our history, such as and not limited to:

1. The birth-life-death cycle.
2. The mind-body-soul connection.
3. Positive – Balance – Negative speaking humans & life from a philosophy trackable since the 14th century B.C.

Throughout history, there are several views about the number three shared in several Myths & Mythologies, such as and not limited to:
It symbolically, represents a portal:

1. Window one to view into another world.
2. Window two to view an inner world such as into our soul.
3. Window three serves as a barrier, a place to view the world but unable to participate.

There is a view about the 3 windows speaking time:

1. Window one is to see the past.
2. Window two is the present.
3. Window three the future.

From Biblical manuscripts, it guides believers to reflect with the following:

1. *"Your eyes are windows into your body. If you open your eyes wide in wonder and belief, your body fills with light.*
2. *If you live squinty eyed in greed and distrust, your body is a dank cellar.*
3. *If you pull the blinds on your windows, what a dark life you will have!"*

How about the number 3 with movies and television shows:

1. Main core characters often come as a *3-pack.*
2. A series will often be a *3-pack.* (If not three, five it will be)
3. Beetlejuice – Beetlejuice – Beetlejuice! - or - how about the Genie with 3 wishes allowed. For the Friends sitcom enthusiasm, at the show opening, each character appears 3 times back-to-back.

How about sports:

1. Baseball: 3 strikes and you are out.
2. Boxing: Be taken down 3 times in a single round and it is a Knockout (KO)
3. Ice hockey: It is a 3-period game (overtime if needed)

How about the following perspective about *time* and the number 3:

1. Theoretically, we should sleep 1/3 of the day. (1/3 X 8 hours = 8 hours X 3 = 24 hours)
2. Theoretically, for many countries, hourly employees work 1/3 of a day. (Same math as above)
3. What is factual, a new season every 3 months! (3 months X 4 = 12 months = 1 year)

Brands stick to people's mind with the *Rule of Three*:

1. Use three words to tagline short punchy and easy to remember.
2. Use three colors in the brand palette for a cohesive and recognizable look.
3. Structure your brand stories in three acts; A beginning, middle, and end.

Let me share one more. There are also expressions, common human behaviors, and marketing with the number 3 (not limited to):

1. Expression: Never 2 without 3.
2. Behavior: Knocking 3 times.
3. Marketing: Buy 2 get 1 free. Also, the number 3 is a power tool in Marketing.

Psychology suggests that 3 is the ideal number for your brain to retain from visual material. The brain finds it easy to grasp threes - elements, colors and fonts – in visual material. When that number is increased to four variables, the brain gets confused. With an understanding and view of our past, the number three therefore works surprisingly great to persuade in business, and our personal life to scale priorities. And persuasion, when a leader of the heart, is a must.

When sharing my inspiration from Stonehenge earlier, I briefly introduced the following principle composed of the following *3-pack*: *Master File – Journal – Communicate.* When this principle is practiced, consistently used/applied, you focus & simplify your message because you understand it, and when you understand something, you explain it simply.

1. Three bullet point summary.
2. Top 3 opportunities/recommendations.
3. Top 3 performance/performers.

Another approach with persuasion and the *3-pack*; if you have more than 3 to share, break them down into 3 categories, and have 3 for each category. In psychology, it's referred to as *grouping and containing*, here's an example:

I worked in retail for several years in the field of Loss Prevention, and per my books, my approach was not by policing – rather – it was by engaging with positive emotions. *Guinea pig* stories will be shared later about the following hidden psychology using persuasion to engage with positive emotions by leveraging *semantic network* for an efficient *classical conditioning* by *establishing similarities.*

In retail, physical inventory accuracy is a must for a healthy replenishment process, and like any business, making sales is critical. A Loss Prevention (LP) professional work with their operations partners, and these partners speak & listen with the following *3-pack,* sales, profits, and customer experience.

Therefore, in persuasion, those key words work like a *scheme* to influence buy-in, engagement, and to add value to the role of a Loss Prevention professional. Yes, it is political. One of several ways I applied my *3-pack* principle; *Mater File – Journal – Communicate,* was by monitoring activities with every assigned location cash registers.

For inventory accuracy, what comes in at receiving must be accurate, and what goes out (at the register) must be accurate. Weekly DATA was saved by type of actions at the register (category) in my **Master File.** Then, I would review the DATA by category by filtering a Top 3 performance / Bottom 3 performance and **Journal** my review for the cash register operator.

When completing field visits, I would make usage of my DATA analysis to influence, coach, and mentor with Standard of Operation Procedures (SOP) with what negatively influenced inventory accuracy and make sure to include what would influence an increase of sales by supporting the sale programs. That is the **Communication** tenant of the principle. Visit reviews were shared with an email summary. Here's a generic.

Sales (Category one)

- $$$ result/observation – coaching/mentor – opportunity
- $$$ result/observation – coaching/mentor - opportunity
- $$$ result/observation – coaching/mentor - opportunity

Inventory accuracy (Category two)

- $$$ result/observation – coaching/mentor – opportunity
- $$$ result/observation – coaching/mentor - opportunity
- $$$ result/observation – coaching/mentor - opportunity

Recognitions (Category three)

- $$$ result/observation – coaching/mentor – positive outcome
- $$$ result/observation – coaching/mentor – positive outcome
- $$$ result/observation – coaching/mentor – positive outcome

The above generic example is to be viewed and understood with the view of an eagle. It is a big picture, pieces of a puzzle, and intended to inspire a persuasive approach to trigger positivity with topics that could easily trigger negative emotions. In short, the messaging was simplified, focused, and sought an interest in speaking thoughts.

Wherever the number 3 shows up in your life, it is generally an omen of creativity, communication, and *positive curiosity*. These three words following my travels, investigation, and philosophies inspire me to share and recommend you, to add the number 3 in your toolbox.

The *guinea pig* experience

Like what is everything shared with my books, including your current reading, the truest means for humans to feel & understand something is by experimenting with it. Have you tasted the ananas before attempting to sell their juicy & sweet refreshing taste?

Here's why this anchor matters:

You can present the most brilliant fact in the world, but without emotion, it's forgettable. Wrap that same fact in a personal story, and it can stick for years. The reason lies in how our brains encode memory.

Neuroscience shows that emotionally charged events activate the amygdala, which strengthens memory consolidation in the hippocampus (McGaugh, 2004). Simply put: we're wired to store emotions, not isolated information. That's why you might recall an embarrassing high school moment in vivid detail yet forget yesterday's meeting notes.

Stories trigger multiple brain regions, not just language areas, but sensory and emotional circuits (Mar, 2011). This creates context, and context transforms raw data into meaningful experiences. Without context, facts are like loose puzzle pieces; with them, they become part of a picture you can't unsee.

For example, saying "My favorite color is blue" will vanish from someone's mind almost instantly. But say, "My favorite color is blue because my mom wore a blue sweater when she hugged me as a kid and that color makes me feel safe," and you've given them an emotional anchor. They'll remember it, because they're not remembering the color, they're remembering how it feels.

If you want someone to remember your belief, lesson, or product, don't just give them the facts. Give them a story that makes them feel. That's the only way it survives in their mind after you stop talking. And those stories are harvested from your *guinea pig* experience.

Like for the book you are currently reading. And *sooooory,* this anchor is a *pratfall,* it's the 16th anchor!

Royalty free picture by pineapple-supply-co-174667

6

Inner sweetness & shell Emotional Control & Management

Emotions are built, not just felt and if you don't control your emotions, they will control you.

Planet Earth has a master shell to protect life:
Its inner sweetness.

Earth quality of life can be defined as:
Emotions!

Earth quality of life – emotions – can be defined by how negative & positive they are experienced.

The influencers for negative & positive emotions are:
Humans!

Emotions, 24/7, every human has them and feels them. It is like a never-ending rollercoaster which contains moments of goodness and displeasure. Society's emotions are another rollercoaster, a wild ride. We could say it is two rollercoasters crossing path frequently. Many things happen every day to everyone, making the management of emotions a challenge.

- A portion of society is controlled by their negative emotions.
- A portion of society turns negative emotions into violence.
- A portion of society chooses to be blind to what facts are. (Cannot handle the truth)
- Political decisions will be felt to be both positive and negative.
- Media will provide positive emotions to a society and sometimes, feed the negative with negative.
- Social media can contain misleading information, "fake news" and personal diary to be seen by all in a life comparison. All these trigger various emotions.
- A portion of society will experience satisfactory emotions by creating traumatic emotions to others.
- And much more can be stated.

Based on the *Pareto principle* (the 80/20 principle), the above list may involve an extreme 20% of society resulting in 80% challenge in remaining positive. The reality is, 100% of society will feel and manage emotions differently making living complicated.

The objective of this chapter is to inform of the challenges you will likely be confronted due to human' emotions, provide perspectives – principles – concepts – and tools. Following your reading of the roots of a pineapple, let's build a few walls (pineapple shell) with the purpose of containing and protecting your inner sweetness (emotions). But first, here's a high-level perspective about our timeline.

An exceptionally long time ago

A topic generating various emotions is religious beliefs. This perspective IS NOT to be Religious. Rather, the goal is to take a perspective trip back in time and, at a light speed, bring us back to now.

Let us remove from our mind all names and stories used in religious beliefs and work with the raw concepts provided in many of them. Could we consider there was already a strong knowledge of humans' emotions thousands of years ago?

Raw concepts from religious beliefs provide guidelines of behaviors and manageable methods for positive emotions leading humans to behave with best practices between them. We could suggest the mission was to establish a positive Culture with Core Values such as: Trust, Respect and Communication.

Globally, every type of religious concept leads to a positive Culture with Core Values.

Each village and town had a representative to help and guide the population to maintain a solid foundation of each concept. There was even at least one day of the week dedicated to it, with an assigned location to congregate, discuss and provide support. The idea of life after death was used to influence best practices by all.

As years went by, the population increased, some individuals took an opposite direction to feed their own emotions regardless of others, generating an overload of negative emotions, dominating, and dividing society with how to manage their emotions with skin color, gender, sexual orientation. In addition, darker challenges came in play; alcohol, drugs, gambling, money, and sexuality are some examples.

Through time, the rollercoaster of emotions became an intense ride. Books of rules with punishments were created in the attempt to influence order and best practices in society. One of the challenges of today is to have a general harmony in society. The list of actions that would most likely influence this objective may be extensive, but we cannot ignore the fact that each citizen of Earth is 100% responsible for how they think, act, and speak. *Soooooory*, but yes, you own and no one else will do it for you!

Though, with the knowledge that perfection is myth and cannot be truly achieved, what if reaching excellence was possible?

Time Management – The seed

Time is not just a clock, it's a mirror. It reflects how we manage our emotions, our energy, and our attention. And *soooooory,* but answers aren't found around. They're found within.

To master time is to master the self. It requires self-control, self-awareness, self-reflection, and focus. These are the roots that cultivate emotional clarity. Without them, time becomes an emotional illusion, a blur that confuses logic and digs a gap within. And many experience effectiveness problems without being aware.

Effectiveness isn't about effort. It's about direction. It's about energy spent with clarity and habits repeated with reflection. Without it, life feels short because we waste so much of it.

Time is one of the five essential elements of The Pineapple Theory: like an Infinity Stone. For centuries, time has conditioned society with an economy obsessed with speed. "Time is money," they say. But time is also emotion. It's the Monday excuse. It's the stress of urgency. It's the anxiety of delay.

Me: "Hey, how are you today?"
Person: "Well, you know… it's Monday."
Me: "I'm sorry, I didn't know Monday was an emotion."

Like the pineapple, which ripens five to six months after flowering begins, everything blooms in its time. The sun and moon shine when it's their turn. And when you protect your time - through timely changes, planning breaks, and emotional boundaries - you begin to see why your timing is perfect. Why things had to happen the way they did to guide you to where you were meant to be.

You can't deny this: If you do the right things, the right things will happen to you. But the right things often take time.
And patience makes kings because pineapples don't grow from magic beans. Don't expect fast results. Always keep moving no matter how fast because as long as you keep moving, there's progress.

Time is emotional.
Don't let time become your roadblock.
Don't let it become your anxiety.
Don't let it blindfold you from what's right.
Don't make it your excuse for poor behavior.
Pause.
Keep it sweet within and around.
Savor your pineapple one sweet bite at a time.

Good etiquette is the glue of society, and it must not be served like American fast food. A society glued together is one that supports and respects. It nurtures a fruitful life experience.

When time is understood and mastered, it becomes your protector. Like the pineapple shell, it shields your inner sweetness. It helps you stay rooted.

Sooooory, but life never pause and time never waits for anyone because it's always moving forward. And through time, many wise minds have spoken. Have we listened?

Lao Tzu
To say, *"I don't have time"* is to say, *"I don't want to"*.

Socrates
Beware of the barrenness of a busy life.

Stephen R. Covey
The key is not to spending time, but to investing it.

Jonathan Estrin
The way we spend our time defines who we are.

Leo Tolstoy
The two most powerful warriors are patience and time.

It's not about having time; it's about making time. To support the philosophic perspective about this chapter along with upcoming topics, remember that if you can see it, you can manage it. When many speak about time being their problem, chances are – and *sooooory* for rambling again - they have an effectiveness problem.

Complementary on my website is an *Emotional Profit & Loss tool.* If a P&L is used in business to challenge and improve financial results, why not challenge how you invest and spend your emotional energy?

thepineappletheory.ca

Time – Protect your time. Define your priorities

If you don't protect your time, someone else will use it for you.

Every time you say "yes" to something that doesn't move you forward, you say "no" to your own future. People will keep taking until nothing is left. And *sooooory,* but your "yesses" don't make them love your heart, they love your hand.

You don't need to answer everything. You need to make space for yourself. Set boundaries fast, like anchors in people's minds. People respect what you protect. If you protect your time, they'll adjust. If you don't, they'll step over you without even noticing.

Here are time management tools to protect your time and define your priorities.

<u>It's OK to say NO!</u>
When keeping focus with what you are aiming for, every minute and hour will influence tomorrow, the next month, the next three months, and so on. Though, even if it takes time to harvest something fruitful, it doesn't mean you are wasting your time. In perspective, never sacrifice your daily 7 or 8 hours of sleep, plan time to eat, plan time for your *daily feel good* (also known as *daily emotional booster*). About the remaining time, choose wisely how you invest it.

The 3-peak performance
Daily, you will experience three peaks of performance.

- The first is your highest for which, requires planning the biggest task and top focus. For me, it's when I wake up because my mind is fresh and sharped from a good rest. That's when I spend from 3 to 4 hours writing.
- The second is a midday peak. Smaller then the first second peak, it's your midday momentum.
- The third is often a late day, much smaller peak. For me, I schedule conference calls and I network.

Between each peak, clear the small things that easily pile ups; your emails, things you can complete in under 5 minutes, returning a call, take 5-10 minute to walk and greet people.

The 3-3-3 Method
The *theoretical 3* fundamental anchor comes in play with this method, and it suggests spending three hours focused on a single task. Then three smaller tasks that take about an hour each. This technique reduces distractions and allows for a more structured work routine.

The 8-8-8 Method
This method focuses on a work/life balance. It suggests to breakdown your day (24 hours) into 8+8+8 hours to make a good balance sheet of your life.

- 8 hours of work.
- 8 hours of good sleep.
- 8 hours spent on 3Fs, 3Hs, and 3Ss:
    - 3Fs are family, friends, and faith.
    - 3Hs are health, hygiene, and hobby.
    - 3Ss are soul, service, and smile.

Prioritization
When working on *Worldwide Fruitful Travels with a Pineapple*, many said, "You should totally go to…" But their suggestions were emotional, not reasoned. *"I'm from (Country), and because we produce the best pineapples there is, are you planning to go?"* is starting with why. Being *positively curious* is the anchor, and cue.

Prioritization required sacrifice. I had to respond with the "why" it didn't fit, and many heard it as a *sooooory* moment.

Start with why. It reframes how you engage. It activates reasoning. It's the *Ulysses Rule*: protect yourself from distractions. Like Ulysses sailing past the sirens. Here's an example:

I built a score-based matrix to prioritize my travel targets. Example:

- Is there a book fair or fest?
- Can pineapple history be found?
- Is there a peculiar pineapple place nearby?
- Does my preferred airline fly there?
- Can I partner with hotels or photographers?

This matrix works in life and business. Give higher scores to tasks that affect your manager's visibility. Use it to delegate when there's a lot of heavy chewing at the same time, use the Ikea Effect, people will be part of the solution. Think of it as avoiding the Eye of Sauron. Here's a very high-level generic example:

	Bookfair 2:Exhibit 1:Visit	Book history 2 : Yes	Attractions 1:Low, 2:Medium, 3:H	Social Media 1 poor to 5 great	Air Travel 2:Direct 1:Not	Hotel 2:Partner 1:Not	Checkpoint 1:Low, 2:Medium, 3:Gi	Total
London	2	2	3	3	2	?	3	17
Tokyo	2	0	3	3	2	2	2	14
Hong Kong	1	0	3	3	2	1	3	13
Edinburgh	0	2	2	3	2	2	2	13
Malina	1	2	2	2	2	2	2	13
Hawaii	0	2	2	2	2	2	2	12
Singapore	0	0	2	3	2	1	2	10
Taiwan	1	0	2	2	1	1	1	8
USA	0	0	2	2	2	1	1	8
Mexico	1	0	2	2	1	1	1	8
Australia	1	0	1	2	2	1	1	8

Many people are taught the *Eisenhower Matrix*, also known as the Urgent-Important Matrix. It's a task management tool that helps prioritize tasks by categorizing them based on their urgency and importance, allowing you to focus on what truly matters.

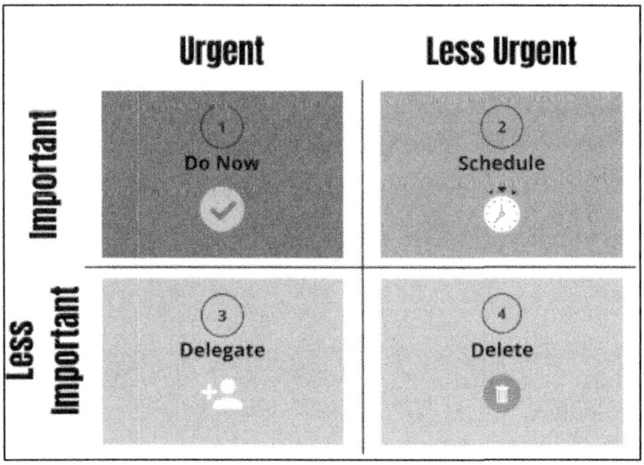

What if you could include a score system in each category? What I personally enjoy with the score system proposal is that everything is on one list, and the weight of each score will define what is Urgent-Important.

These tools support the *7 fundamental rules* for time management, and they cultivate positiveness.

- It helps plan your day with goal setting.
- You organize yourself because of your habit to journal, which is best practice to de-clutter your mind and equilibrate your emotions.
- You reduce the risk of multitasking because you have a focus, meaning goals with datelines and time limits.
- It assists with (1) removing distractions and non-essential tasks because (2), you have wisely prioritized.
- You wait less for the perfect time to do what is important, and you have between cycles for the easy things.
- Lastly, you can plan your work-life balance ahead, and please don't forget planning time for the unexpected, and take breaks between tasks for a quick boost of your *emotional batteries.*

Sooooory, but in life, you can do anything, but you cannot do everything. Focus. Expect people to critic and see the decision you made, not the choice you had.

A seed about timely changes

I have three indoor plants, my COVID plants. Weekly, I water them for long-term blooming result, and they remind me of time, growth, and emotional cycles.

Lucky Bamboo
We can live with the thought that everything in life is a miracle or with the thought that our results are from our hard work. We can think about our dreams, but to make them happen, we must act with one definite step forward towards them, never stop moving, no matter how fast because slow progress is progress.

My Lucky Bamboo is a reminder of our success because for the first five years, nothing seems to happen on the surface. But then, almost overnight, it shoots up to 30 meters in just a few weeks.

What we don't see is that during those years of stillness, bamboo was quietly building a deep and resilient root system underground. Without that hidden foundation, the sudden and impressive growth above ground wouldn't be possible at all.

The same principle applies to everything we set out to achieve. We put in the workday after day and see no results. But if we persist - not with motivation (because it fades), but with consistency - success often seems to happen overnight. In reality, it's the effort we invest during those invisible seasons that builds the foundation for breakthrough. Bamboo waits five entire years before it rises. And in a technological era that conditions you expect fast results, it's no surprise you feel ready to give up after just a few months.

My Lucky Bamboo also reminds me of trusting my roots. Honor your pace. And remember growth that lasts is always built underground first.

White Orchid
My white Orchid reminds me that life is a cycle with Ups & Downs. From blooming to the fall of its flowers. From a new branch growing to blooming again. My white Orchid consistently changes following each cycle. It never stops growing, and it always finds its way to bloom.

Like us in life, we cannot outgrow ourselves, and we need to always cultivate a growth continuum within making us bloom. No matter how much we take care of what is external to ourselves, what is external will show signs of aging but within – our inner sweetness - remains beautifully fruitful.

My White Orchid also reminds me to always take care of yourself because you are your greatest worth. Invest the time and profit positivity and health from your daily investment.

Purple Orchid
Lastly, my small purple Orchid. The last time it bloomed was 3 years ago. Often shared, there aren't no magic beans. Don't try to rush a process.

My purple Orchid reminds us that the easy road often leads nowhere and that the difficult one leads to what is right. It requires consistency, and your consistency is your determination.

Always cultivate like a farmer, you may not see instant results, never quit with yourself. Difficult does not mean impossible. Do the right things and the right things will happen to you. Like being consistent at nurturing the small purple Orchid and seeing it blooming 3 years later. It exhibits a big heart full of hope even if soon, like the white Orchid, will remind me of the cycle also reminding u to never stop because there's always more blooming days ahead when it's cultivated.

To conclude, when I'm told that Orchids are likely the most challenging indoor plants to keep blooming, if you don't limit your challenges but challenge your limits instead, and if you Believe to Achieve, there's growth.

Japanese culture
Oubaitori, meaning, the idea that people – like flowers – bloom in their own time and their own individual ways.

<u>Change</u>
When there's a change, I suggest there are 3 types of people:

The *"proactives"*
They prepare. Kaizen.

The *"reactives"*
They adapt, complain, then adjust. It's often a 3-month process.

The *"stubborns"*
They resist until they are forced because they are no longer able to change a situation. Then, they are challenged to change themselves. They are reminders that only a fool never changes their mind. If they don't, they resist life.

More about installing a new habit with this book. For now, to build new habits, try:

- **17 repetitions** for long-term memory
- **30 repetitions** for short-term impact (*Mega-Drilling effect*)
- **21/90 Rule**: 21 days to build, 90 days to reinforce

Writing about change, myself though, have my comfort zones. Does it mean that I'm afraid of change? The answer is no, and when it's about a physical change, I will apply visualization with the purpose of anchoring a seed in my mind. It's an interpretation of a psychological concept referred to as, *The Commitment and Consistency Principle*, and here's an example of its application and what it suggest.

In the 1970s, a psychologist conducted a famous experiment with the purpose of understanding why people say, "yes", even when they don't want to. In one test, a researcher approached strangers on the street and asked them to put an ugly oversized "Drive Safely" sign in their front yard. Almost everyone refused, but then they tried something different and a week before, they asked another group to put a tiny harmless sticker in their window that said "Drive Safely" for which almost everyone agreed. Small, easy, insignificant. Then, a week later, the researchers came back with the same ugly sign. This time, 76% of people said, "yes" and here's why?

Their brain had already decided, "I support safe driving." Saying "no" now would be inconsistent with who they believed they were. This behavior is *The Commitment and Consistency Principle,* and it suggests that once people make a commitment, they tend to act consistently with that commitment, even if their initial decision is later revealed to be flawed. This principle highlights the human tendency to justify their choices and actions to maintain a sense of self-consistency, which can lead to people reinforcing their original decisions, even if they are not optimal.

Let's get back on track with questions to myself: Will change sometimes require my self-control within to keep control about what I can control, meaning adapting to change with positive solutions and attitude? The answer is you bet!

Without changing our thinking, we can't change the world because life is a process of our thinking. Every emotional comfort you currently experience was once an emotional discomfort, then from a continuum of changes, and continuum of improvements.

If you put yourself in a position where you must stretch outside your comfort zone, then you are forced to expand your consciousness to strive and achieve. Everything is hard before it is easy. Nothing in this world could be done without change, including your growth.

To speak more perspectives about your comfort zone, never forget that you are the captain of your life, and you may find that your ship is safe at harbor, but it's not what it was designed for. Meaning that, if you don't move, you'll never notice the chains holding you back. You always have the power to shape your future.

Change takes time and not everyone re-directs with the same artistic ability. For many, being anchored the thought about a change ahead or eminent, will often be the source of anxiety because it's viewed as a problem, and the solution is like a tool we never used before. It is a challenge to experience positive emotions when we are giving our attention to one or many problems. Truth be told, giving it attention makes us the problem because all solutions are seen as problems – or – there is a problem for every solution. There is no minimal sign of active listening. It is like a pigeon picking the ground. It is like driving and changing lines without looking at your blind spots. It is like walking in public head down at a cell phone. Philosophically, if a problem triggers anxiety and there's no solution, is there truly a problem? From our timeline, wise voices have spoken to inspire people to take control of their anxious emotions with the purpose of seeking solutions.

Confucius
When it is obvious that the goals cannot be reached, don't adjust the goals, adjust the action steps.

Dalai Lama
Look at situations from all angles, and you will become more open.

Bruce Lee
The knowledge and skills you have achieved are meant to be forgotten so you can float comfortably in emptiness, without obstruction.

What we think being obstacles are often a creation of our own making and good news; our thoughts are also our cure and *placebo*! If you apply life's *Law of Balance*, anxiety triggered by a roadblock can switch to emotional control if you change how you act & view that same roadblock. It reminds me of the 1998 movie, The Waterboy, when Coach Klein wins over his anxious challenges because he chose to view his roadblock – his adversity - differently by giving it a baby face. In perspective, Coach Klein became productive with his anxiety, and it took him time to become agile at using with confidence, his tool.

Productive Anxiety
Often ramble, emotions are built, not just felt. Humans do have strong emotions for their patterns and change to their patterns will trigger negative emotions. Additionally, what could be a potential change, thinking about it, or when *forced* to apply a change will likely trigger anxiety. It's a feeling about never being able to do enough, often experienced in the workplace when no recognition is provided from one's hard labor and the reverse, when there's not enough to do and we are becoming anxious to perform.

What if one could benefit from their anxiety to become productive? In psychology, it's referred to as, *Productive Anxiety*, and it suggests generally amounts to worrying about things you do have the power to change.

Hopefully with this book, you will be able to practice a few tools to thrive when anxious, and among psychologists, there are seven best practices to turn anxiety into productivity:

1. Use its adrenaline.
2. Reframe your anxiety.
3. Accept that anxiety may be inevitable.
4. Channel the anxiety into motivation.
5. Distinguish productive worry from unproductive worry.
6. *Decatastrophize* your anxiety.
7. Practice centering.

Productive Anxiety can escalate and become *High Functioning Anxiety,* typically refers to someone who experiences anxiety while still managing daily life quite well. Generally, a person with *High Functioning Anxiety* may appear put together and well-accomplished on the outside, yet experience worries, stress, or have obsessive thoughts within.

This, I must share, not only is a person wearing a mask, but it also drains their emotional batteries and the habit of journaling de-clutters the mind to keep better control of their emotions.

Also, when you bear in mind that you don't know what someone is going through within, a zest for *positive curiosity* when interacting with them speaks is emotionally intelligent. Cultivate this mindset:

Imagine meeting someone who takes time to truly know you. Someone who listens - not to judge or correct - but to understand.

Your past. Your experiences. Your perspectives. They ask with care. They speak with respect. They act with authenticity.

Now imagine: What if you could be that person?

As generational cycles accelerate through technology, we must not let speed undo our ability to think. We must not let convenience replace connection. Because in life, most people assume others are fine, but they're only glancing at the surface. In truth, many are living their hardest moments alone. Not because they want to, but because no one noticed the cues. No one activated their positive curiosity. Unless you're positively curious, you won't know:

The silent struggles someone carries.
The project quietly fueling their ambition.

The mindset shaping their day.
The feedback they're afraid to share.

Challenge yourself. Swap "How are you?" for "How are you today?" And when someone says, "I'm great," follow up with: "That's awesome; what's making your day great?"

From there, something emotionally boosting will start to emerge. Because when you ask with care, you don't just learn. The fastest way to be interesting is to be interested. You love through Respect, Kindness, Good Manners, and good etiquette.

Stress Management

Pineapple fruit is a sweet & exotic dessert. You also, can be a "dessert." Who has never said or heard about someone: *"Ah, he's/she's so sweet!"*

Many stressed people will - without noticing it - mirror their stress to you and your stress may also be mirrored towards others. It's *Darwin's Theory*. That is when your *pineapple shell* - your protector, per my theory - can protect your inner sweetness and your inner warrior's greatness by remaining positively focused on achieving several objectives & goals efficiently. If not used, you are letting your inner sweetness being fed by others' negative emotions, and your own. Then, you start becoming someone you are not. The *Superego* lives. I also suggest that stress is like the Devil, and its Demons are fears, shame, worries, concerns, and lack of self-confidence or self-worth.

In life, use your fundamental anchors of *positive curiosity* by *seeking within* because they will assist you to better understand the roots of things to cultivating solutions and harvesting growth. From my careful observation with humans' emotional patterns, I suggest the following top 5 categories acting as a cue for stress, and the observation is a self-assessment tool to pinpoint the root of your stress.

(1) Time
Time hunts again when giving negative attention to a past that no longer exists, a future that does not exist, and the conditioned pressure from our technological era for which, nearly anything & everything must be available - or happen - now.

The past and the future is out of your control; don't stress yourself too much with it. And when you manage your time properly - and are organized – you break free; it's a stress killer. Keep focus.

(2) Stressed about an unknown upcoming result.
In reference, it's like *Schrödinger's cat,* a thought experiment that illustrates the paradox of quantum superposition, suggesting that until observed, a quantum system (like the cat's fate) exists in a combination of states (both alive and dead).

It's a *curiosity gap* for which the gap can only be filled once the outcome is made available. Though, like the cat, you have the choice to face this situation positively, negatively, or both. Only one can truly energize your *emotional batteries* with the purpose of remaining anchored.

When I originally wrote my unpublished title, *The Pineapple Theory – Theoretically the Origin*, I suggested a perspective called, *the leftover*. Our brain has this instinct to view extremes, like winning or losing - a positive or negative outcome in this case - and we must train ourselves at adding a third alternative with the purpose of reducing our conflicting thoughts – the *dissonance* – by giving them an anchor. Meaning, the cat is both alive and dead.

What I have suggested with *the leftover* is often, the size of negativity we have built and making its way through all the layers of our *pineapple shell* may not be as big as it is. We supersize it from our own thinking. Let's give this view an image with a Simpson break and enjoy the following YouTube clip before moving on with my motion of thoughts.

In the clip, what was a threat broke and only a small piece burst through Earth's pineapple shell. The *leftover* was small, and with positiveness when looking at it, there was nothing to be worried about. Maybe it's the result of you being a genius, meaning you've prepared to fight adversity, also referred to as being proactive. A tool of the thoughts with the purpose to reduce conflict between extremes is to see it to manage it. Here are pragmatic applications:

I was providing mentoring to a client who kept seeing problems impacting their inner sweetness. All roads of potential solutions for *positive curiosity* with were immediately converted into a problem. Therefore, I proposed the following exercise:

Journal: Write down each problem, only their roots. Besides each, write the simplest solution and what you're ready to give up. My client took an evening to reflect and complete the exercise. The following day, my client was recharged with positive energy and self-confidence because no matter what the outcome, solutions were made available.

An episode of the popular sitcom The Big Bang Theory served the audience with a valuable approach when stress consumes an unknown upcoming event. Raj was stressed out because he was waiting for confirmation about the space probe, he worked on to respond. Following failed attempts at seeking an anchor to reduce his inner conflict, he drove his best friend Harward to a Hinduism Temple. You see, being disconnected from yourself is a reason for stress, or stress became the reason to disconnect you from you. It's a misalignment. Therefore, an inherited location anchored in you to recalibrate your inner peace is a power tool to consider even if you are not a believer because meditation breaks free – it's a stress killer - because these buildings are built to let air breathe and generate good energy.

(3) Stressed by fear of being caught for our dishonest, wrongdoing, or immoral act. The solution must be engraved in your mind as follows; do the right things and the right things will happen to you. Though, and from several people I investigated with the purpose of being *positively curious* about their dishonest behavior, good people make mistakes. Meaning that, nearly everyone on this wicked planet likely once did a wrongdoing for which consequences would have been hurtful if caught.

Be in control of your emotions because you may think you're a good person, but take away your comfort such your food, your security, your stability and you'll see how quickly your morals vanish morality. It is universal, it's a privilege, and the moment survival is at stake, the mask comes off.

Under extreme pressure, the *prefrontal cortex,* the part responsible for morality, gets overridden by the *amygdala* which only cares about keeping you alive. Suddenly, what was once unthinkable, becomes logical. You lie, steal, betray, and your mind justifies it, not because you're a bad person, but because morality was never about truth. It was about what was convenient.

If you want to know who someone truly is, don't watch them when they're comfortable; watch them when they're desperate because pressure reveals character faster than time. This is how you identify who you can trust and who will betray you. Though, never betray yourself, and you will never betray around.

(4) Stressed for our action for which, we feel shame.
This one I find interesting because it's stressed out of self-built shame for doing something right but against conditioned perceptions. Here's a story of mine about it.

On 22 January 2025, Amazon announced the cease of all their First-Middle-Last mile operations in Quebec, an impact for 3,500+ people. I was a Regional Manager with them, I had launched all their Last Mile facilities, and I decommissioned them. That's a full end-to-end cycle.

Being out of work at 42 (in 2025), with 25+ years of experience along with being an Indie-Author makes the search for a new job a challenge, and because a broken heart and empty pockets teaches you the best lessons, I increased my level of frugality. Career and job ambiguity is another cue for stress.

In February 2025, the Quebec Government launched an update of their recycling program; an aluminum can return credit increased from $0.05 to $0.10, and a drinkable plastic bottle of 250ml to 2L from $0 to $0.10.

My daily feel good is weightlifting, and I don't miss a day at the gym because exercising is another stress killer. Additionally, to combining passion, hobby, and exercise, eating healthy joins the fun which is one more stress killer. What if I told you that daily, I collect cans and bottles gym members leave behind, and that each month, what I have collected covers more than my monthly gym membership fee? In fact, the total amount received is non-taxable, I move the funds into a tax-free account. Then I receive a 20% tax credit when submitting my annual tax report and inject my tax return into the account. Then, I let the magic of compound help me earn more. I call it *Free money.*

That's only from one daily workout. At first, I felt stressed and shame for sneaking ways to collect as many units as possible. But why? Am I acting without morals, or am I simply being smart? It is behavior against a conditioned view by others because what they see is someone picking from the trash bin, only if they see it because once again, I found ingenious ways to collect them. Because my action make sense, the best way to free myself from shamed stress is to activate my *Default Mode Network and* tell myself *"fuck it"!*

Giving attention to our thoughts about what we do not control is a waste of our emotional energy, and when stressing ourselves about what people think of us - if we do what is right and logical because others have not thought of it - the best way to break free and kill the stress is to tell yourself *"fuck it"!*

Another topic to consider about shame is the concept of losing face. *Lose face* began life in English as a translation of the Chinese phrase *tiu lien.* That phrase may also be expressed in English as *to suffer public disgrace* - that is - to be unable to show one's face in public.

In the Chinese Culture, losing face is said to be caused by embarrassment, disagreement, or criticism. *Losing face* is equal to losing the respect of others and avoiding this situation - saving face - is very important in the Chinese culture.

In the Japanese Culture – thus - even someone who is higher than you in the hierarchy is ok to disagree with. However, Japan, along with other Asian cultures, has the concept of "face" (*mentsu*). To disagree with someone in public, thus causing them embarrassment, is to make them *lose face.*

In Asia and India, losing face can be experienced when one declines one's good action based on one's values. Example: Declining a person's offer to pay the check at the restaurant, declining a gift, declining a person's assistance to help, and more.

In North America, shared like a scenario: She was afraid that she would lose face if she admitted her mistake.

One's individualism culture blind spot is one having excuses for everything thinking one is *saving face.* One thinking is *saving face* makes others *lose face.* Efforts to *save face* - among psychologists - lead to a *loss of face.* One is thriving with good manners in this world when they understand what is *losing face.*

The one who made one lose face was one thinking for themself. An extreme obvious of public disgrace was witnessed by the world on 28 February 2025 when US President Trump and VP Vance erupted at Ukraine's President Zelensky.

The Pineapple Theory's philosophy reminds us that it starts with you because it's not about you, and you are a thriving gift when you understand it's not about you. You are a bigger gift to the world when you are stronger than your ego because your ego is your biggest enemy; it doesn't care about you, nor about others.

(5) Stressed in the workplace

Like cats, kids love playing with empty boxes. It becomes their vehicle - fort - castle. With in mind that adults have an inner child, the box is a mental & emotional feeling. It is sometimes the making of their own mind, often fed by others and/or the making of others, and it becomes an environment. In the emotional illusions with *life & time*, beliefs of a grown one will be lived as if they were in a box, without seeing through it.

With the engraved thought tool of making the right things for the rights things to happen to us: Commit to the laws – Commit to a company's Procedures and Standard of Operation (SOP) – Commit to all Safety regulations and procedures.

Everything within those limits; make it fun, stress free for yourself, and others. If the environment does not want you to have fun, move on, change your environment. The kidder Garden or School is not suited for you. Let your inner child have fun in the box. Here's a list of stress cues in the workplace requiring working with the tools on hand with this book, talk with your manager for solutions, or self-assess your own leadership.

- Too much to do at once.
- Random interruptions.
- Constant change.
- Mistrust, unfairness, and office politics.
- Unclear policies and no sense of direction.
- Career and job ambiguity.
- Poor feedback; constructive or challenging.
- No appreciation.
- Lack of/poor communication.
- Too much or too little to do in general.

Lastly before we harvest this topic, if being stressed feels like a roadblock, reshape your roadblock and give stress a baby face by reading stressed backward because it will become sweeter. Remember that the person who can handle stress is the one who can handle success and thrive because success isn't just about winning, it's also about rising through challenges pushing forward when it gets tough. Master your stress and success will follow. And stress is needed in our life, and here's why:

Your mind is a tree: Why stress is essential for growth

What if I told you that your mind is exactly like a tree?

In the 1990s, scientists constructed a sealed ecosystem known as Biosphere 2. It was designed to mimic Earth's biomes - deserts, oceans, rainforests - under ideal conditions. Within this utopia, trees grew rapidly. They appeared strong, tall, and healthy. But then, something unexpected happened: they collapsed under their own weight.

The reason? No wind.

Wind, it turns out, is not just a nuisance to trees, it's a necessity. It acts as a form of stress, prompting trees to grow deeper roots and develop stronger trunks. Without it, they lack the internal structure to support themselves. They break, not because they're weak, but because they were never challenged to become strong.

Now consider your mind.

Philosophically, we often seek peace by avoiding discomfort. But avoidance is not peace, it's stagnation. In Stoic thought, adversity is not the enemy; it's the forge. Marcus Aurelius wrote, *"The impediment to action advances action. What stands in the way becomes the way."* In other words, resistance is the path to resilience.

Psychologically, this principle is echoed in the concept of *eustress*; positive stress that motivates and strengthens us. Without it, we don't build coping mechanisms. We don't develop emotional muscles. We remain fragile, vulnerable to collapse under the weight of our own untested thoughts.

The Pineapple Theory reminds us - supported by psychological concepts and philosophical patterns - we learn that to truly observe who someone is, we must see how they respond under stress. Because often, when pressure mounts, morality becomes a myth. The mask slips. The roots - or lack thereof - are revealed.

Your mind, like a tree, needs wind. It needs challenge. It needs friction. It needs an occasional storm. Not to break you, but to deepen your roots. Not to weaken you, but to strengthen your core. Hard times aren't just helpful for growth; they're essential. They shape your character, refine your values, and reveal your capacity to endure. Without them, you risk becoming a beautiful structure with no foundation.

So, the next time life sends wind your way, don't curse it. Lean into it. Let it shape you. Let it remind you that growth without resistance is hollow. Because the mind, like the tree, doesn't flourish in perfection. It flourishes in truth. And truth, more often than not, arrives with wind.

9 Coaching Actionable Items

1- Wind Mapping: Identify three recent challenges you've faced. For each, ask:

What emotional muscles did this test?
What value did it clarify?
What root did it deepen?

2- *Eustress* Inventory: Make a list of activities that stretch you, but don't overwhelm you. These are your "wind workouts." Schedule one this week (e.g., public speaking, cold outreach, deep journaling).

3- Root Reflection - Ask yourself: What beliefs or habits keep me upright when life gets stormy? Write down three. Then ask: Are these roots deep enough? What needs strengthening?

4- Storm Simulation: Choose a controlled challenge, something you've been avoiding. Step into it intentionally. Reflect afterward: Did I bend, break, or grow

5- Mask Audit: Recall a moment when stress revealed something unexpected about yourself or someone else. What did you learn? How did it shift your understanding of character?

6- Pineapple Lens Practice: Using The Pineapple Theory, observe someone under pressure this week. Don't judge, just notice. What does their response reveal about their emotional structure?

7- Marcus Moment: Each time you face resistance this week, repeat: "*What stands in the way becomes the way.*" Let it guide your response, not just your reaction.

8- Biosphere Check-In: Are you living in a sealed ecosystem of comfort? Audit your environment:

Are your conversations challenging?
Are your goals stretching you?
Are your routines too predictable?

9- Make one intentional change to invite "wind" into your week.

Listen to your emotions

In life, if you kindly listen, it means you are actively listening. Learn and cultivate this habit, it truly becomes the essence of your intelligence. I mean, it is taught with the basics of economy that in life, nothing is free. Truth must be told about that because indeed, nothing is free in life, not even learning because you must pay attention.

Often shared with my books, the wises spoke and no one listened. If someone can speak to your emotions - about your mistakes from your thinking, actions, and speaking - actively listen and follow their voice like a treasure map. Don't let your foolish ego harm you by persisting in your own self-deception and ignorance.

Don't listen to respond, listen to understand because it cultivates growth. Don't just hear questions you are able to answer, *be positively curious* if you don't have the answer, that's how you grow within. When someone has answers to everything, it's often because the right questions are not asked.

Many people are challenged at reaching the attainment of their greatness because they don't listen to the way they respond to questions and situations. Their mind is blind to their reactions. Hearing you speak cultivates awesome thriving greatness because it's the act of *seeking within* with *positive curiosity* to always improve. You see, you may notice a change in the attitude of others, and my mentorship question to you is, have you noticed a change in your behavior that made them change? It starts with you.

Emotional Granularity – See it to manage it
The reason why people are often overwhelmed by their emotions and why they can't control them is simpler than you think. They don't listen to or name them accurately.

In psychology, it's called *emotional granularity*, and it suggests that people with a rich, nuanced emotional vocabulary are better able to regulate their emotions, they are more resilient to stress, and they are at a lower risk for certain mental health conditions compared to those who use broad, generalized terms like "bad" or "good" to describe their feelings. But those words are like blurry photographs; they don't help us see clearly. High *emotional granularity* is considered a skill that can lead to better emotional and social wellness, and it begins with naming emotions precisely. It's like sharpening the lens on your inner camera. Here's a simple guide to expand your emotional vocabulary:

- Instead of *"I feel bad,"* try: Disappointed. Ashamed. Overwhelmed. Lonely. Restless.
- Instead of *"I feel good,"* try: Proud. Peaceful. Energized. Connected. Curious.
- Instead of *"I'm stressed,"* try: Pressured. Anxious. Frustrated. Distracted. Overstimulated.
- Instead of *"I'm fine,"* ask yourself: Am I content? Am I numb? Am I avoiding something? Am I quietly hopeful?

The more precisely you name your emotions, the more power you have to manage them. It's like switching from a blurry pineapple sketch to a high-definition image of your inner sweetness. And when you name it, you name it.

The main driver behind emotions is the *amygdala,* whether it's negative emotions like fear, or positive ones like love, because that's where the activity happens. The *amygdala*'s counterpart is the *prefrontal cortex*, the part of the brain responsible for logic complex thinking and rationality. Exactly what we need.

When our emotions spiral out of control, neuroscience shows that when a person clearly and precisely label their emotions, they activate the *prefrontal cortex* and reduce activity in the *amygdala.* That's how they regain control over their feelings.

If emotions remain vague and undefined, the brain interprets that uncertainty as a threat, triggering more anxiety and confusion. If a person creates safety, it converts threats into manageable data for them. This means learning vocabulary, just like in school.

Naming is claiming. And when you claim your emotions, you don't just protect your sweetness, you give it space to bloom.

Anger
When anger takes over someone's emotions, it becomes a powerful emotional domination over one's true self. It requires practice to quickly snap out of it before acting with anger which will lead to several regrets becoming more negative emotions. Like the first half of Hulk's life.

Most often, when feeling anger, it means that something needs to change. For about 30 to 60 seconds, deeply breath inside/out and seek your fundamental anchors. If your environment makes you angry, step outside the environment, walk to cool off and repeat the process; for about 30 to 60 seconds, deeply breath inside/out and seek your fundamental anchors.

By moving locations, such as going for a walk or switching from the living room to the kitchen, you break that emotional association. You create a neutral ground, where fresh perspectives can emerge without the baggage of prior tension. Legal systems recognize a similar concept through *"cooling-off"* periods: a delay or physical move gives people critical mental distance, preventing impulsive decisions or emotional responses. Even walking through several door frames assist this process. In criminal law, and because emotions are easily anchored to their environment, the *cooling off* process by walking through doors often assist in determining impulsive or premeditated crimes.
Every time you do not act with your anger, you rewire your brain to become calmer and more compassionate. It's neuroscience.

And if someone becomes angry over silly or petty things, the common pattern is they need love.

Wise voices from our history have spoken with the purpose of preventing us from acting with our anger.

Epictetus
Any person capable of angering you becomes your master.

Dalai Lama
If you can, help others. If you cannot do that, at least do not harm them.

Confucius
When anger rises, think of the consequences.

Socrates
Do not do to others what angers you if done to you by others.

Frustrated
Before raging like Godzilla or reacting like a Monkey, understand that you are likely stuck. So, deep breath for about 30 to 60 seconds. Step away from the problem while enjoying a juicy sweet pineapple bite to keep your conscious thoughts busy and let your non-conscious take a lead. Then, re-engage with the problem. Chances are you will see it differently.

Remember, there's more than one way leading to the top of the mountain so try a new way and if you can't think of a way. Be *positively curious* and seek someone else's perspective because there are always solutions, if not, is there truly a problem?

Guilt
You did something that doesn't match your values. When someone tells you something they did not appreciate about what you said or how you acted with them, it is a gift because it may give light to something that does not match your values.

Every time we plan to give something, it must be viewed like a gift, and like a child, what makes a gift a positive experience for our inner child is how it was given. Often, an apology is the solution. Like the gift of a pineapple because it's welcome. Always leave on a positive high note like what is falling asleep without remorse, it's a thriving path to wisdom.

The 3-5-7 Apology Methodology
If and buts are not an apology! It is like always having excuses for everything. Pointing fingers is easy and emotionally lazy. It is the roadblock to self-awareness and growth. The easy road leads nowhere. Pause and reflect.

What I suggest with the *3-5-7 Apology Methodology* is that it cultivates your emotional intelligence. The experience becomes efficient from an eagle view, with minimal biases, to imagine and structure each step of the *3-5-7 Apology Methodology*.

Emotionally, it is very difficult to admit to ourselves how we could have done or said differently preventing the need for an apology for someone else's actions. The Apology process is valuable because if it's needed, it likely means that how we have decided to think, act, and/or speak to someone else's actions was not efficient. It means we could have done better. We can only improve. When efficiently applied, you can feel your growth. It can also become a lesson-learning for the recipient and the giver. What is a gift for someone keeps on being given to others. That is a powerful influence. When you pause and reflect, which bucket is best suited to give an apology like a gift? A friendly tip: Beware of the *time* blind spots.

The 3-step Apology methodology
1. I'm sorry.
2. This is what I did.
3. This is what I am doing to correct it.

The 5-step Apology methodology
1. Name what you did wrong. Own your actions.
2. Use empathy. (Emotion : Emotion)
3. Make it all about you because it's not about you.
4. Brief explanations.
5. Let it go. (Refer to the *Let it go principle*)

The 7-step Apology methodology
1. It's prompt. Name what you did wrong. Own your actions.
2. Agree with the facts. (Find common ground/commonality)
3. Take responsibility.
4. Explain what you did wrong.
5. Express regret.
6. Make it better.
7. Explain why it won't happen again.

Your emotions are not interruptions. They are invitations.

The Theory of Empathy

What if the following top 5 is experienced by highly Emotional Intelligent people?

(1) They talk to themselves because talking to yourself helps you think better and solve problems more easily. True when writing because when you can see it, you can manage it, and written words are the mirror of your non-conscious and soul.

(2) They have a high sense of humor, enjoy jokes, and funny things because they become more creative and better at handling difficult situations. Like the sun, they shine & thrive when people laugh and are more attractive & fruitful when they speak about the things they truly are passionate about. Laugher is also truthful.

(3) They like solitude because spending time alone helps you think deeply and learn more about yourself. Always take time to understand your passion and values. Always make time for things, making you happier. If you feel alone in the most difficult times of your life, that's not weakness. That's the season shaping your wisdom.

(4) They are open-minded. Being open-minded means you're willing to consider new ideas, which can help you solve problems, and come up with thriving new things.

(5) They have high observation skills, noticing and understanding things well, which helps you at making better decisions and to always understand the world around you better. In life, you can have excuses or solutions, not both. Since complaining is not

a habit, they inspire solutions instead of just talking about problems. Focusing on solutions helps you to become more proactive and make positive changes.

Reading books nurtures a reader's Emotional Intelligence because they Read-Think-Relate. Their reading is not only for information, but also transformation. It's more than reading words, they train themselves in listening to words and looking into your eyes meaning that they may not say a lot, but they do notice everything.

They read moods.
They read energy.
They read vibes.
They read body language.

But some people in the paradox of Advance Emotional Intelligence. In psychology, it is said that some people find it almost impossible to fully hate or dislike someone even if they've been hurt by them.

Why?

Because their brain instantly shifts into that person's perspective. This isn't just being open-minded. In fact, it's a sign of advanced emotional intelligence rooted in something called *cognitive empathy.* It's the ability to understand another person's perspective and mental state on an intellectual level, without necessarily feeling their emotions. It suggests a capacity for perspective-taking, or "putting yourself in someone else's shoes," to understand their thoughts, feelings, and intentions. This understanding is a key component in social cognition and helps in building relationships, negotiating, and predicting behavior.

"How could they do this to me?" instinctively is *"what must have happened to them for this to make sense?"*

But here's the hidden cost. *Law of Balance.* The same gift can blur boundaries because when the brain is trained to understand every angle, it can start justifying patterns that should never be tolerated. They explain away red flags until hurt feels normal and harmful behavior feels predictable.

So, tell me, is deep empathy your greatest strength, or the reason you keep getting hurt?

Never forget yourself. Never lose yourself. What you inculcated in yourself you can only see in others because you have secured yourself enough to play with fire of others.

The sweetness within is now rooted. What comes next is the crown—the mastery of the mind.

7

The Crown
Mastery of the Mind

**Where your mind flows, emotions goes.
Be in control of your mind and you'll be in control of your life.**

Where's Waldo with a Pineapple in the Matrix?

What if I told you that your mind is your power tool, the connector grouping together your roots, foundation by keeping it solid, your emotions because they require supervision, and how you consistently care, train, and use your mind will give what is defined per The Pineapple Theory as your authentic pineapple crown?

You may have told yourself once (or more) or have heard others dwell by sharing they do not have the mental capacity or strength to face challenging situations with themselves. *Sooooory*, but what is difficult is not impossible.

A nutriment for success with your mind is how you choose to speak to yourself because of being the person you will talk to the most in life. Everything you tell yourself will wire your self-belief about who you truly are. *Soooooory* again, but no one thinks about you more than you do. Your mind is your cure for everything and it's also your *placebo.* Your negative thoughts lie to you and lies hate to be challenged, keep challenging for positiveness & self-confidence for the win. With repetition, if you control & supervise your emotions & thoughts, you will think more clearly because your mind can easily become an illusion. If you regularly educate yourself at always understanding the reading of your mind's blueprint, you then upgrade your mind's software to fit today's fast evolution of our reality. In perspective, change how you think and use your mind, and you will change your reality. Think of a movie projector. Here's a serving of psychology about this paragraph before resuming with more analogies, metaphors, and philosophy.

A lie repeated a thousand times becomes the truth. This quote is nurtured from the leading propaganda minister of 1930s Germany, and we all saw just how effective it was in shaping and manipulating society. Repetition has the power to rewire the brain. This is based on the *illusory truth effect* which says that the more often information is repeated, the more likely we are to accept it as truth regardless of whether it's factual which is why ads, rumors, and catchy slogans stick with us.

This process is driven by *neural priming.* Every time a thought is activated, the brain makes it easier to access meaning that the more you hear a certain idea, the quicker and more automatically you'll recall it until it becomes part of your belief system.

Also, there's the *mere exposure effect*, which is the simple act of repeated exposure making us more comfortable with the concept even if we don't consciously know why. The brain connects repetition with familiarity and familiarity with truth.

With The Pineapple Theory's philosophy that *Being Kind & Truthful makes like Life much more Fruitful,* if you want to change someone's mind – and yours - don't just tell them once but keep repeating the idea. Over time, their brain will make it their own truth.

This is why your crown must be consciously sculpted. If you don't shape your mind, the world will. And what settles in your crown becomes the lens through which you see everything.

In psychology, the following are referred to as:

- The *illusory truth effect,* also known as the *illusion of truth,* describes how when we hear the same false information repeatedly, we often come to believe it is true. Troublingly, this even happens when people know better, that is, when people initially know that the misinformation is false.
- *Neural priming* suggests that prior exposure to a stimulus influences subsequent responses to that stimulus or related ones, even without conscious awareness, leading to faster processing and potentially more efficient decision-making.
- *Mere exposure effect* suggests that people develop a preference for things simply because they are familiar, meaning repeated exposure to a stimulus, even if fleeting, can lead to increased liking or preference for that stimulus.

What was still is with our timeline. Since thousands of years humans are fed and they keep feeding themselves with several Myths & Mythologies with the attempt to live life, as humans, emotionally better by understanding life & themselves better through their philosophy and stories. Time always moves forward, humans' population never stops increasing, and several forms of Myths & Mythologies exist to emotionally reach humans' core, meaning, their emotions like there are several superheroes.

Understanding life and humans emotionally better is sometimes positively influenced by perspectives surrounding us every day. Allow me to share an observation inspired by my 2023 trip to Tokyo with a text called, *Theoretically History with The Pineapple Theory.*

To better understand life and human emotion through history, I've often shared - and demonstrated in this book - that everything in today's timeline has an origin. It's a growth continuum: what was becomes what is. Our timeline is not linear. It's a looping continuum of becoming.

For example, following New York's 9/11, Earth experienced a reset with the air travel security process. It's an *extreme obvious* which insightfully gives light to question our timeline about its reset from the 625BC to 476 AD era.

The *what was/still is* perspective suggests – in part - that humans' emotions are well known for tens of thousands of years. Maybe not medically at that time, but emotionally because of behavioral patterns. You see, our brain is skilled at detecting patterns, and it's a skill most people don't know they need or have. In 2015, Neil deGrasse Tyson quoted the following:

"Over centuries of evolution, humans' pattern recognition skills determined natural selection. Hunters skilled at spotting prey and predator and telling poisonous plants from healthy ones offered them a better chance of survival than those blind to the patterns. It enabled the survivors to pass on those pattern-friendly genes to future generations"

We can't help it. Our brain craves patterns *(Bor, 2012)*. With our ongoing fast evolving technological era, for example, if we can turn data into a pattern or rule, then according to Daniel Bor, *"near-magical results ensue. We no longer need to remember a mountain of data; we need to only recall one simple law"* (Bor, 2012).

We all have an innate ability to recognize patterns, it's deep rooted within, and this makes us the positive solution for everything because we have always been the solution in life. Even in our technological era, for now, we have the technology to capture data, but we do not have the technology to analyze it. For tech savvy, this may not last because a computer algorithm has not yet been developed that outperforms the human mind to analyze data and detect patterns. Again, from this book, I suggest that technology must evolve, but it must not undo humans' ability to think. Self-awareness therefore is of our own power to detect patterns and better skilled in how to harness it puts everyone in reach of discovery and innovation. If you ever watch the 2017 movie, The Founder, Ray Kroc is an *extreme obvious* that shows how everyday people can make discoveries big and small. One pattern detection by Kroc launched the McDonald restaurants which today is one of the most successful fast-food restaurant chains in the world.
A special layer of the brain found only in mammals is responsible for pattern recognition. It is called the neocortex, the outermost layer of the brain. Because of its numerous folds, it accounts for 80% of the weight of the human brain. According to Ray Kurzweil, the basic structure of the neocortex is organized around groups of neurons called *pattern recognizers* estimated to number 300 million. Over the course of a lifetime, Kurzweil proposed that these recognizers can rewire themselves to one another to account for the new visual, number, nature, word, and people pattern we learn over time *(Kurzweil, 2012)*.

Your crown isn't fixed; it's fluid. Every pattern you recognize, every thought you repeat, every truth you challenge, rewires the crown. That's how you evolve from reactive to regal.

Pattern recognition with open eyes for an open mind gives life to the *Law of Balance* fundamental anchor. Previously shared, for every positive creation, there will be the creation of something negative, and for every negative creation, humans are forced to create something positive.

Senso-ji Shrine, Tokyo Japan 2023 - Copyright Steve "Mr. Pineapple" Mathieu - Photographer: Yusuke Harada

Senso-ji Shrine opened in 645 A.D. It is Tokyo's oldest and most iconic Shrine and often observed is a symbol strongly speaking several aspects about humans' emotions with The Pineapple Theory. If repetition can rewire belief, then symbols - especially ancient ones - can rewire emotion. Let's explore how one symbol, once sacred, became a global trigger for trauma, and what that reveals about the emotional software of society.

<u>The swastika</u>
In Buddhism, the swastika is considered to symbolize the auspicious footprints of the Buddha. It is an aniconic symbol for the Buddha in many parts of Asia and homologous with the dharma wheel.

From its history, the swastika symbol first appears in the archaeological record around 3,000 B.C. in the Indus Valley Civilisation. It also appears in the Bronze and Iron Age cultures around the Black Sea and the Caspian Sea. In all these cultures, the swastika symbol does not appear to occupy any marked position or significance, appearing as just one form of a series of similar symbols of varying complexity. In the Zoroastrian religion of Persia, the swastika was a symbol of the revolving sun, infinity, or continuing creation. It is one of the most common symbols on Mesopotamian coins.

The icon has been of spiritual significance to Indian religions such as Hinduism, Buddhism and Jainism. The swastika is a sacred symbol in the <u>Bön</u> religion, native to Tibet.

Haken Kreuz (Gamma cross)
What was a sacred symbol for positivity was then highjacked, meaning that the symbol was slightly modified (flipped/reversed) becoming a psychological conditioning and manipulation to influenced what is negative (evil) to be viewed as something positive.

Theoretically with The Pineapple Theory
This example about the positive & negative from our history showcases the origin of something positive that was modified becoming negative. When WW2 ended, the Gamma cross became a symbol of hate – a huge "no no" everywhere - and the swastika lost its positive historical meaning in most part of the world. The rise of the Third Reich and Germany's entry into WWII put an end to its popular usage worldwide, and the subsequent Holocaust ensured the swastika would never again be utilized in any benevolent sense in the Western world. In fact, it is illegal to display the symbol in some countries (Austria, France, Germany). Japan was influenced to stop using the swastika prior to them hosting the 2000 Olympics, and all other Eastern world avoids its usage largely influenced by the Western culture although there's no law restricting it.

Both symbols were not drawn the same, but they were similar tricking the non-educated eye & mind. Sadly, instead of educating the mind, the easy road was taken by simply removing it, no matter if it's a positive or negative meaning.

I will squeeze the philosophical thought with a sting *soooory* because this situation speaks of today's era. What is negative will often be simply covered rather than being taught to understand, meaning that it's easier to simply remove *what was* the positive about it and let the negative become the last checkpoint in people's mind.

From sacred symbols etched in stone to headlines etched in grief, the emotional patterns of humanity remain unchanged. Whether in a shrine or a city street, the question persists: how do we interpret what we see, and what do we choose to ignore?

A more modern example about the "cover-up" suggestion can be found with a Quebec SUV vs Pedestrians case.

Downtown Montreal, the night of 26 February 2023 at approximately 1830hrs, a 21-year-old skateboarder (victim) was found severely injured on the street due to a hit-&-run. Moments later, an SUV was found abandoned about 4KM (2.5 Miles) away from the scene and confirmed involved in the incident. The victim was later confirmed dead. Sad to hear, deadly impacts on pedestrians, skateboarders, and cyclists happen often in Montreal.

This isn't just about one vehicle or one victim. It's about how society responds to discomfort by pointing outward instead of looking inward. The SUV becomes a metaphor for emotional avoidance, and the media's reaction becomes a case study in psychological deflection.

DATA confirms that victims die more often when hit by an SUV (bigger vehicle + law of physics = no surprises). The following day on 27 February, the leader of Pedestrian Quebec was given the microphone by the media and planted the seed that SUVs should be banned in Montreal because they are considered deadly. Then, the media along with TV talk shows started cultivating this thought.

Throughout Earth timeline, there is no hiding or denying, humans are more reactive than proactive. With this emotional understanding, safety & risk mitigations are always needed because humans are often emotionally glancing at what are risks. I can't stress enough the *extreme obvious* example of the 1994 Hot Coffee judgement in the United States.

Are mitigating measures truly the absolute rooted solution?

Would humans' behavior with how they choose to *think-act-speak* becoming a culture be the root cause of about 99% of road accidents?

Why barely anyone is speaking about humans' behaviors with the purpose of inspiring them to *seek within*, teach awareness and prudence becoming positive solutions for their actions?

Rather, there is again a cultivation of seeking around which is the easy psychological road to humans' problems. Sadly, if someone had to speak about human beings' being responsible, it would not be heard positively, many would emotionally be offended because many are conditioned in life to seek around first, instead of within. True if the identity is pointed out. It must be speaking the action.

About the victim: Were they wearing reflective wear, wearing safety gear such as a helmet, wearing headphones with music on?
About the suspect (No matter the type of vehicle): Were they truly focused - texting & driving, falling asleep - speaking on the phone when operating their vehicle and/or, were they under the influence of alcohol or drug?

For this ongoing investigation by Law Enforcement, there are allegations that the abandoned vehicle, confirmed a rental, was likely stolen. Theft in America is another Cultural problem with how society chooses to *think-act-speak*. Even myself, in February 2023, had my brand-new vehicle stolen in front of my house. Additionally, each time I attended a police station and mentioned the client I represented; officers impulsively shared with me: *"Your client is giving us crazy work because people are stealing."* Each time I respond the following, and believe it because it's true, they hate my response: *"The problem is not my client, the problem is society lacking integrity, thinking for themselves, and can't live with each other respectfully. The problem is the roots of society and not by seeking around by pointing fault around."*

In life, both pedestrians and drivers are responsible for their actions to make it safe around, and for themselves. If you did not know, Quebec is the only province in Canada where crossing a pedestrian walk is at your own risk. This is cultural, owned by society. When one is thinking for themself, it leads to nothing positive, like ignoring the safety rules when driving, or as a pedestrian. Furthermore, can you name a country where, once you have received a driver's license, there are mandatory follow up exams? Even with our ongoing modern technology era, developing technology for self-drive vehicles with the hope to reduce accidents is at some point, walking away and seeking around what is within humans. The less society is trained to think by seeking within what are positive solutions with how they choose to *think-act-speak*, the more dead there will be leading to false conclusions, the weaker many humans will become to manage their emotions to a positive level with themselves. And those who *think-act-speak* from a place of good will once more, per the timeline, always be penalized and common sense will not be one's gift, but their sentence.

The "cover-up" view is influenced by time and humans' psychology about their laziness, meaning that in a fast-paced era along with the bareness of a busy lifestyle for which, taking time to pause and reflect about what unfolds is often considered complicated. I have the following analogy in-mind about the "cover-up" suggestion:

It's like a teenager with a pimple on their forehead. Instead of treating it, they cover it with makeup. It looks resolved, but it isn't. A trained mind sees the cover-up… and the avoidance behind it.

Sooooory, I will ramble again; we are teaching history, but we do not learn from it. You see, the more technology evolves, the more how humans feel & think moves backwards and humans must not let technology undo their ability to think. Your eyes are useless if your mind is blind because the illusions in your mind will create your life's emotional illusions with *life & time.*

The movie series, The Matrix, suggests life being an illusion. Something we think we know, but don't because like our emotions, it's built. Strip away everything your mind thinks it knows, and you begin to see life, plain. When you see through the illusions, you find yourself. Your true self. And you realize: you've always been the solution. You always will be.

Add viruses to life illusions and they become an emotional distraction emotionally tricking one. If a person once found himself and can identify what life illusions are, one will be able to read & decode the viruses and remove them to protect their peace by returning to themself. If a virus is acknowledged and can't be removed, anti-viruses are available to assist one.

Where's Waldo?
Drawings of perspectives that can be viewed as: We are all Waldo! Can you find yourself and your tools wherever you are?

What was still is.
Life's illusions are always emotionally under attack by viruses to trick one with their thoughts and emotions. This book and creation of The Pineapple Theory are one of many anti-viruses available. One more reason why I suggest that pineapple is an

addition to one's life recipe. It is like an anti-virus of good vitamins, freshness, and authenticity. What is positively authentic is the fruit presented to its simplest, without – or by breaking through - any emotional illusions by using refreshing and authentic principles, concepts, and philosophy.

I was once asked: *"Is The Pineapple Theory Religious or Spiritual?"*

My response was: *"It's a neutral zone, between both to remind everyone of the positive, from their belief, within."*

A neutral zone also exists in The Matrix. Like fruit, one can add the pineapple to another ingredient to level-up their own life recipe because it's zestier. It's like upgrading the software of your anti-virus. And every upgrade strengthens your crown. Not for decoration, but for direction. Because the crown isn't just what sits atop your mind. It's what governs it.

In the Matrix, don't let your mind be your own illusion. The Matrix can be within and around, and so are the viruses. When it is chaos in the Matrix, it must be faced to achieve peace, but can you find Waldo first?

Because the only person a human will speak to the most in their life is themself, in perspective, what if each Myth & Mythology through their stories is sharing to humans' an emotional reasoning process with the purpose of keeping their instinct positively alive with their anchors?

What if the stories of each Myth & Mythology include characters created for humans to investigate within, acting like superheroes, to have someone to speak positively with when speaking to themselves with the purpose of keeping a positive mindset through the characters' stories in similar life events? This suggestion therefore means that those Myths & Mythologies are sharing the following: You got a friend, in you!

In perspective, what if for tens of thousands of years, humans always and still have the liberty to do the right things, freely, even when no one is watching? When many are protesting, asking for freedom, what if their greatest freedom is already available; the one about choosing their attitude and taking 100% responsibility of themselves? The freedom of not letting their poor behavior be their excuse to compensate a barely use freedom of thought.

Like pineapples on a pizza, there is no emotional perfection, laws & books of rules *was and still* are needed to keep an emotional balance in society. After all, what if humans' emotions require supervision with their thinking and reasoning? What if when humans are losing themselves with the positive reasoning of the Myth or Mythology of their choosing, laws & books of rules are needed?

Plato
Good people do not need laws to tell them to act responsibly, while bad people will find a way around the laws.

You've seen the illusions. You've named the viruses. You've walked through the myths and the metaphors, decoding the emotional software of society. And now, you stand at the edge of mastery.

The crown is not a decoration. It's a declaration. Of clarity. Of courage. Of emotional sovereignty.

Every pattern you recognize, every thought you repeat, every truth you challenge rewires the crown. That's how you evolve from reactive to regal.

The Pineapple Theory doesn't ask you to escape the Matrix. It asks you to decode it. To wear your crown with kindness, truth, and emotional clarity and thrive.

Because the mind is your temple, your kingdom, and the crown is your compass. And when you wear it with truth, you don't just protect your mind, you lead it.

Let's keep diving into the mastery.

The Pineapple Theory "Matrix" became an inspiration for my books cover pages, and several views positively feeding its philosophy. One image spoke a thousand words.

Your mind is your Temple – And it wears the Crown

Acropolis – Athens (GR) 2022 - Copyright Steve "Mr. Pineapple" Mathieu - Photographer: Georgios Makkas

The pineapple analogies & metaphors about my theory shared 15 fundamental anchors referred to as the roots of an ananas. Then, the inner sweetness referred to as our emotions along with tools to build multi-layers of the shell, also referred to as the protector. In between, the soil, referred to as the foundation and the containment to navigate on the river of life, allows you to put a roof on, meaning the crown referred to as your mind. Though, building the foundation or your boat will provide you with great lessons. In fact, it's a process requiring sacrificing an old self to become the person you wish to become because if you don't destroy your old self, it will destroy you. Meaning that, your new life is at the cost of your old life, and the only thing standing between you and the life you want is you. Per the wisdom of Myths & Mythologies, it's your resurrection and per Biblical manuscripts, 3 falls are expected before a life changing comeback.

The deepest form of self-care is building a life you're in love with. For many, that feels unbelievable. But the only truly impossible journey is the one we never start. It's making a spreadsheet of your debt, enforcing a morning routine, and cooking yourself healthy meals and no longer running from your problems and calling the distraction a solution. It means looking at your disappointment square in the eye and re-strategizing. It is not about satisfying your immediate desires. Letting go is choosing new. It disappoints some people. It is making sacrifices for others. It is living in a way most people won't so you can live in a way most people can't. It is becoming the person you know, you want and are meant to be. Someone who knows that salt baths and chocolate cake are ways to enjoy life, not escape from it because your inner world follows you everywhere. You are here to always understand yourself better. A valued visual about this philosophy speaking our foundation was witness when I traveled to Athens in July 2022, and it inspired the following.

Athens, Greece: Next to the Acropolis can be found the Acropolis Museum. A structure speaking a thousand words about the importance of a solid foundation to keep a pineapple stable and tall on it.

The Acropolis Museum foundation is built on top of the foundations of several houses founded at the end of the 4th or beginning of 5th century AD. A period of residential prosperity for the area and the whole of Athens. They constitute spacious, although not luxurious buildings, dwellings for the people of the middle class. Developed over the remains of older houses, they were in use until the beginning of the 6th century AD, when new buildings were constructed.

Acropolis Museum – Athens (GR) 2022 - Copyright & picture by Steve "Mr. Pineapple" Mathieu

What I harvested from this visual beauty of our history is that our growth process requires building our foundation as previously mentioned. Everything we do for a first time will likely fail a few times with the purpose of rebuilding on "new grounds" and more solid. This perspective strongly speaks the philosophy of our own resurrection, a process for which people hoped for us to achieve and for which, who we became for the second half of our life becomes our legacy for eternity. Though, it's the opposite of the "cover up" because pieces of the old foundation are still valuable and more important, erasing them would erase the person you are today, and it speaks volume about our history; Learn about history because it will move you forward. The better a foundation is built and the stronger it needs to be rebuilt to succeed with a very important and growing purpose, keep your mind stable because it is your temple.

In the emotional illusions with *life & time,* never lose contact with your temple and the less you will lose and forget yourself. Bear in mind that througout Earth timeline, every Myth & Mythology guided one to at least once a week, to congregate, to meditate. An important process to pause with the purpose of never losing yourself and never forgetting yourself. A time that is not about finding yourself, rather, a time to return to yourself.

Your temple runs on emotional electricity. Every thought is a wire. Every feeling is a current. And every act of kindness is a voltage boost. If you don't recharge, the lights dim. The doors weaken. The foundation cracks.

Frequently visit your temple like you recharge your cell phone. The *daily feel good* comes in play to assist with this process and never forget that your temple is a place that restores your energy, not one that drains it. Inside your temple, a pineapple can be added to make it welcoming with great hospitality for yourself, and others. *Home Sweet Home* for yourself, and a place where others would be pineHapply to come back.

Also inside, stories can be found from your timeline, like our timeline, as seen in several museums. A fun fact about this statement is found at London's Natural History Museum. A world-class visitor attraction and leading science research center. Their unique collections and unrivalled expertise tackle the biggest challenges facing the world today from our past. There are more than 80 million objects spanning billions of years, the museum hosts more than five million visitors annually, and a large portion of the collection are from Naturalist & Geologist, Charles Darwin. Inside the main hall, can be viewed and admired on the ceiling, several hand-painted arts from nature and one pineapple plant can be observed. The fruit is the jewel of the jungle!

Natural History Museum – London (UK) 2025 - Copyright Steve "Mr. Pineapple" Mathieu

Inside your temple, there are artifacts showcased into see-through boxes and they have negative emotions you've experienced; they do not live freely. They are visible to remind yourself from time-to-time of your story, how you evolved, the challenges you surpassed, and more. You see, you will always be home for your demons, and keeping your mind secured and in control is not negotiable because it would be like releasing several ghosts in the city becoming chaos, a reference to the classic 1984, Ghostbusters. Though, if they do escape, *"who you gonna call?"*

Every artifact is a reminder of your past, the person you once were, and exploring is not about living in your past, it builds self-confidence because you have always moved forward making you the person you are today. They are an ongoing understanding about why things had to happen the way they did with yourself, and they propels you to become the person you will become 10 years from now. Each artifact is part of your foundation keeping your temple stable. Walking inside your museum from time to time is considered important to return to yourself, not to lose yourself, and not to forget yourself. Many don't make time for this important walk, or they will sacrifice it first. Until one day, they are forced to take care of an illness, leading to regrets about repeating what was already exhibited.

Seen in the Marvel Studios movies, the negative emotions from the artifacts are calling you, and they are trying to emotionally manipulate you. Never forget that your temple has a door, and you own opening the door to those tricky emotions called by the artifacts inside your museum. You are the "bouncer", and your inner warrior is the guardian of what & who enter your temple and the more Kind, Truthful, in Peace, and Organize within, the more blooming you will attract, speak, and act. If needed, install an oversize sign, inside/out the door of your temple informing you of the following: NO NEGATIVE EMOTIONS ALLOWED!

Your temple is not just a place of memory—it's a place of mastery. And when you guard it with truth, kindness, and clarity, you don't just protect your crown. You illuminate it.

Mentalism and the walls of beliefs

According to psychology, your mind is always searching for proof of what you believe, and your mind will believe everything you repeatedly tell it. When telling yourself that things are always going wrong, your brain will focus on every setback, your mind will focus on every small inconvenience and use them as evidence to confirm that narrative. It's not that life is objectively worse. It's that your brain is doing its job. Seeking to reinforce the story you've chosen to tell.

This is explained by *The Principle of Mentalism*: "The All is Mind; the Universe is Mental."

This ancient Hermetic principle isn't just mystical poetry; it's a psychological blueprint. It suggests that everything begins in the mind. Before action, before habit, before identity, there is thought. And if the universe is mental, then our inner world isn't just a reflection of reality, it's the architecture that shapes it.

In coaching, this principle becomes a call to radical responsibility. If your thoughts shape your experience, then you're not just reacting to life, you're co-creating it. Your mindset isn't a lens. It's a lever.

Psychologically, this aligns with *Cognitive Behavioral Theory* and *Self-Schema* models: we act in accordance with who we believe we are. The stories we tell ourselves aren't just narratives; they're neural instructions. Every belief becomes a behavioral script. Every thought becomes a rehearsal for reality.

This is why *Positive Curiosity matters.* It's not just about asking questions, it's about reclaiming authorship. When you stay curious about yourself, you keep rewriting the script. You expand. You evolve. You refuse to settle for survival when expansion is possible.

Mentalism invites us to become mental alchemists, transmuting fear into insight, judgment into compassion, confusion into clarity. It's not about bypassing pain. It's about meeting it with awareness and choosing to respond rather than react.

This is also why the *Law of Balance* is important because it flips narratives. It reframes them. If you start asking yourself, how can things get better, what good is happening in my life?

Your brain will begin to look for those answers. It will seek out the small victories, the moments of growth, and the opportunities for change. The more you do it, the more your thought habits thrive, and the more blooming and fruitful life's experience. The positive approach to seeking self-authentication is water for growth, incrementally shifting your perception toward hope and possibility.

In psychology, it's referred to as *confirmation bias at work,* and it suggests that an employee or manager tends to actively seek out information that supports their existing beliefs or opinions, while ignoring or downplaying evidence that contradicts them, potentially leading to flawed decision-making and a limited perspective on issues within the workplace.

Per The Pineapple Theory's fundamental anchors, *I think; I assume; I believe; I guess* are cue words to become *positively curious* because the cues are proven to not speak facts, and being *positively curious* must be deployed with the purpose to discuss thoughts, ideas, and challenge assumptions. It doesn't have to be negative, but your mind is doing what it's wired to do, meaning finding evidence that supports reality and what you believe in. And if you don't challenge your beliefs, the taller the walls surrounding you, and logic can no longer be seen.

The habits of your mind, your thought process, is your cure and *placebo.* You are your thoughts because your thoughts are you eventually becoming your actions. A kind reminder that in psychology, it's referred to as *Ideomotor theory,* and it suggests that a thought or mental image can trigger a seemingly reflexive or automatic muscular reaction, even without conscious intention, and that actions are represented by their perceivable effects.

In life, you will always harvest what you planted. Always be mindful of the story because you are writing the narrative, you create shapes to the lens through which you see your life. Be intentional about how you frame your experiences because what you tell yourself today will become your world. An *extreme obvious* and application about this topic is found with my title, *Worldwide fruitful travels with a pineapple,* as follows:

With our ongoing era of the timeline, without a fully regulated nor truly in-control with the evolution of A.I., biased information and disinformation are fed daily, making self-growth books with philosophy to nurture HOW – and not what - one can think like mine are a must for everyone. Lengthy again with this book, I strongly suggest that the evolution of technology is a must, but it must not undo humans' ability to think. Here's a small example about what I suggest, observed on September 2024 on Instagram (IG), and proving the impact of social media when people don't use their logic when trapped in their belief, and when they blindly applaud what they emotionally see. An IG user shared the following with a clever animation acting like a concept calld, the *shiny effect,* meaning, distracting one's inner child's focus, like an illusionist does with magic.

"1-year = 12 months
12 months = 52 weeks
52 weeks / 4 = 13 months

Why are we then paid for 12 months when there's 13 months? 😟 "

A frequently observed conclusion is that my logical truth will be removed if I comment with these users, as follows about the above: *"If you're paid weekly, you are paid 52-weeks and if you receive a bi-weekly pay deposit, there's 2 months in a year with 3 deposits, meaning that "13th month".*

Sharing a logical truth will shock people deeply trapped in their beliefs because there's no more logic. Sad to say, brutal pain is often what awakes them, speaking once more about the *guinea pig* experience. Somehow, the following story inspires me to not debate with them, meaning that in life, one with knowledge chooses silence as the tool of a great warrior because no war is engaged.

Don't argue with Donkeys!

The Donkey once said to the tiger, *"The grass is blue."*

The Tiger replied, *"No, the grass is green."*

The discussion heated up and the two decided to go see the Lion, the king of the jungle. Even before reaching the forest, where the Lion was sitting on his throne, the Donkey began to shout, *"His Highness, is it true that the grass is blue?"*

The Lion replied, *"It is true, the grass is blue."*

The Donkey hurried up and continued, *"The Tiger does not agree with me, contradicts me and annoys me, please punish him."*

The king then declared, *"The Tiger will be punished with 5 years of silence."*

The Donkey jumped up happily and continued his way, happy and repeating: *"The grass is blue!"*

The Tiger accepted his punishment, but he asked the Lion: *"Your Majesty, why did you punish me, after all, the grass is green."*

The Lion replied, *"Truth be told, the grass is green."*

The Tiger asked, *"Then why are you punishing me?"*

The Lion replied, *"It has nothing to do with the question of whether the grass is blue or green. The punishment is that it is not possible for a brave and intelligent creature like you to waste time arguing with a Donkey, and on top of that to come and bother me with this question."*

Let's harvest this story with the following perspective strongly speaking insights from my books: In life, one of the worst wastes of time is to argue with the fool and the fanatic who does not care about truth or reality, but only about the victory of their beliefs and illusions. Never waste time with arguments that make no sense because there are people who, no matter how much evidence and proof we present to them, are not able to understand, and others are blinded by ego, hatred and resentment, and all they want is to be right even if they are not right. In perspective, when ignorance screams, intelligence is silent. Your peace and quiet are worth more.

Mentalism reminds us: the mind is not just a mirror. It's the maker. And when you choose your thoughts with clarity, you don't just shape your beliefs, you sculpt your crown. So, let's keep sculpting.

London (UK) 2024 - Copyright Steve "Mr. Pineapple" Mathieu – Picture by Hozir Sahdat

Thrive Fearlessly

In 2020, I feared, and still, I clicked. Fear is not the end. It's the invitation. And when you answer it with courage, you don't just survive, you thrive. Fearlessly.

My first book was self-published in a world with likely more titles than there are readers. I was not an author, no one knew me - and likely still not as you are reading this - and I had tons of excuses feeding power to my fears because there are always excuses to not do something. And *sooooory*, but excuses are a myth, here's why:

Excuses are a self-protection mechanism, not a strategy for success. Psychologically, they function as a form of ego defense, specifically, *self-serving attribution bias.* This bias leads people to attribute failure to external, unstable factors - "I was tired", "it wasn't fair"- and success to internal, stable traits – "I worked hard". It helps maintain a positive self-image but undermines accountability and performance (Miller & Ross, 1975).

In the framework of *Self-Determination Theory* (Deci & Ryan, 1985), autonomy is a key driver of motivation and success. Excuses rob you of autonomy. When you externalize responsibility, you also relinquish control. Your brain stops planning for success and starts preparing for emotional damage control which ironically increases the likelihood of failure. That's not psychological safety; it's preemptive defeat. In psychology, it's *Predictive Processing Theory*; run weak prediction in your mind, and your life will be weak.

This is compounded by *Self-Handicapping Behavior* (Jones & Berglas, 1978): if you don't give your best, you have a fallback story. But the cost is steep, reduced effort, impaired growth, and chronic underperformance. The world doesn't care if your reason is legitimate. Outcomes are judged, not intentions.

The corrective strategy here is cognitive reframing. It's once more the *Law of Balance.* Reframe attention from "why I might fail" to "why I could succeed." This tap into approach motivation instead of avoidance motivation. You train your brain to expect reward rather than prevent pain. A subtle but powerful neurobiological shift involving the dopaminergic reward system especially the mesolimbic pathway and nucleus accumbens.

The result? You're no longer preparing to survive shame. Per my deposit bottle story, *"fuck it".* You're preparing to succeed, and that changes your behavior, your effort, and eventually, your identity.

Since that day I clicked and self-published my first book, moving forward was, and is, the only option. What was the goal? At the time, I wasn't sure, and that's because the tip of the hill was too high to be seen. Like at ground level and trying to see the tip of Mt. Everest; it's likely blurry and unclear. I was myself learning from my own theory and product making me the *guinea pig* of my own theory.

Every time you face a fear, you polish your crown. Every time you finish what you start, you rise into it. It is only by starting the journey that you pave your way somewhere and are achieving milestones becoming a step for the next one. Less blurry it becomes, you start aiming at something because of defining goals, each becoming new stepping stones and self-motivation to keep on going.

It's like when I'm in London and walk into a castle's main hall. A first step, then a first pillar (milestone), followed by a spread of stairs leading somewhere higher, and becoming more beautiful. It's the same with a flower bursting through the soil, the more it grows, the more it blooms. Even when many think it's impossible, never forget that a spring flower grows when there's snow. What is difficult is not impossible, and you can achieve the impossible if you cultivate your greatness, start doing, and finish what you start because stalkers fade, starters disappear, but the one who finishes is remembered.

London (UK) 2024 - Copyright Steve "Mr. Pineapple" Mathieu – Picture by Hozir Sahdat

Since 2020, I made challenging decisions with The Pineapple Theory books, and I often adjusted & fixed several things – like my manuscripts - from time-to-time to keep them fresh and tasty. In fact, the more I was *positively curious* about self-education, my travels, and research, and the more through my books I experienced the *Imposter Syndrome*. In psychology, it describes an internal experience where an individual suggests that despite having clear evidence of their competence and success, they are unable to internalize their accomplishments and instead feels like fraud. They live in persistent fear of being "found out" or exposed as inadequate, often attributing their successes to luck, charm, or external factors rather than their own skills and effort. So, the more I kept harvesting refreshing perspectives, and the more I felt The Pineapple Theory was a fraud, and each manuscript update following a book event had a cost in the first 5-years of Authorship.

I know the recovery from these updates increased the challenge to re-install trust from the first sets of readers because they've anchored a reading experience from titles that were not yet ready to be truly harvested – my Imposter Syndrome thinks that - and here's a word of the day speaking of this: Inchoate, and it describes something that is not, or not yet, completely formed or developed. It's like harvesting a pineapple from its catkin when it does not take form properly. Let's add a cherry on my pineapple like on a German Toast Hawaii. My books do not follow the standards meaning that they are not readers' typical books. That's another fear I must surpass because it's not easy to present something different in a world of conditioned standards, in a world consistently making you someone else. People will always try to put you in a box but must build your own. Meaning that, being consistent and facing your fears becomes one of your greatest accomplishments.

This book is an example of the fruition of how my work matured; I broke free from the *Imposter Phenomenon* and new seeds are always being cultivated in my pineapple plantation.

At book fairs, like at the London Book Fair and Frankfurt Book Fair, vendors and people from the industry recognize The Pineapple Theory stand, and they come to share a *"hello"*, take pictures, seek inspiration from my speaking, purchase a book, and sometimes make a deal.

Most importantly for me is that I'm meeting awesome people. My greatest feeling is when I exhibit because wherever I go meeting the public, I must not fear to spread a message of human values, spread a message of harmony, empowering people with their life, and the most important becoming the greatest inspiration for this book: Inspire people to conquer their inner wars, cultivate their seed for greatness, and live more pineHapply by adding a pineapple to their life recipe.

But being in the spotlight requires breaking free from what might hold you back. For example:

Many hold themselves back from opportunities - from posting, from speaking up - because they think everyone's watching, waiting to judge. But psychologists call this the *Spotlight Effect* (Gilovich, Medvec, & Savitsky, 2000). It's the tendency to vastly overestimate how much others notice and remember our actions. Here's the truth: most people are too preoccupied with their own insecurities to care about yours. Previously shared with this book; no one thinks of you more than you. What feels like a catastrophic mistake to you - stumbling over words, wearing the wrong shirt, awkward silence - barely registers for others, and is usually forgotten within seconds. The brain inflates self-awareness and projects it outward, making you believe scrutiny is harsher than it actually is. Once more, the *Law of Balance* becomes the solution, it reframes.

- Reframe judgment: When the fear hits, remind yourself: people are focused on themselves, not me.

- Start small: Speak once in a meeting, post one video, test one idea. Each action trains your brain to see the "spotlight" vanish. It's eating a pineapple one sweet bite at the time.
- Build visibility: Success demands attention. You cannot be remembered if you keep hiding. The illusion of judgment disappears the moment you consistently act despite it.

People must break free from self-doubt. It's not a flaw, but a maladaptive coping strategy. Psychologically, repeated self-criticism often functions as a form of *Self-Handicapping* (Jones & Berglas, 1978). This is when your brain creates preemptive justifications for potential failure – "I'm not good enough" or "I'll probably mess this up" - to shield their core self-worth if things go wrong. It's a way to preserve ego integrity by blaming failure on lack of ability or effort, rather than facing full emotional exposure. And yes, *sooooory*, I repeated *Self-Handicapping,* it was needed.

Neuroimaging studies show that this kind of inner dialogue activates regions like the *medial prefrontal cortex* and *Default Mode Network*, areas linked to *self-referential processing* and *rumination.* Over time, these thoughts become habitual and automatic. Your brain gets efficient at sabotaging you, not because it hates you, but because it thinks it's protecting you from emotional pain or social rejection.

But there's a catch: this "protection" destroys performance. Research on *self-efficacy* (Bandura, 1997) shows that believing in your capacity to act is one of the strongest predictors of success. The more you doubt yourself, the less likely you are to persist, take risks, or even start.

Cognitive diffusion can free you; it's a core skill in *Acceptance and Commitment Therapy* (ACT). You learn to separate yourself from your thoughts. A powerful technique here is visualization: picture each self-critical thought as a physical weight or chain and visualize yourself dropping it. This engages the posterior cingulate cortex (linked to mental imagery and identity shift), helping your brain embody the new perspective. Like Sheldon Cooper's "drop the pen" visualization scene in The Big Bang Theory (S14E4).

On the other side of fear, there's more than what you seek, freedom is also found. And *sooooory*, but most people don't want freedom, they want comfort. They say they crave independence, but the moment life hands them full autonomy, they collapse. Freedom sounds appealing, until it becomes obvious that it means having no one left to blame but yourself.

From a psychological standpoint, freedom is not just opportunity, it's also burden. Autonomy requires confronting your own limitations, your lack of discipline, and the weight of full accountability. When there's no external structure - no boss, no parent, no institution, no Inherited Path - you lose the convenient targets for blame. And with that, you lose your psychological safety net, and for this context, it's known as *Deathground Strategy.*

This is where Julian Rotter's *Locus of Control Theory* (1966) becomes essential. People with an external *locus of control* believe their outcomes are dictated by circumstances, fate, or others. They say things like "The system is rigged" or "It just wasn't the right time." That externalization reduces internal stress but reinforces helplessness. Those with an *internal locus*, on the other hand, accept that success or failure is a direct result of their own choices. This mindset is harder, it removes excuses, but it's the only one compatible with genuine freedom (Lefcourt, 1991).

Most people unconsciously cling to structure not because they need direction, but because they need someone to resent. Structure gives them built-in excuses: "I couldn't because of work," "I failed because the rules weren't fair." But when you're truly free, those excuses evaporate, and what's left is you. Your habits. Your discipline. Your character.

Last one is breaking free from the fear of losing. In psychology, it's *Loss Aversion.* Losing hurts twice as much as winning feels good. Your brain is hardwired to avoid loss at all costs. And this fear might be holding you back more than you realize. Think about it, why do you hold on to things - bad relationships, jobs, or habits - long after they stop serving you? It's because the pain of letting go feels worse than the potential gain of moving on. And *soooooory*, but the truth is, the biggest risk is not taking one. When paralyzed by the fear of losing, ask yourself, "what if I would gain twice as much from leaving as expected, would I still hold on to this way?"

Remember that when there's fear, there's a task, and growth doesn't come from playing it safe. It comes from embracing the risk and possibility of something better.

In you, there's a seed of greatness, cultivate it, and expect challenges while doing so. I'm rambling again; it's difficult, but it is not impossible. Challenge your limits and be consistent because it defines your determination. Believe to Achieve.

Since I took my first definite step forward and published my first book, I feel free within and I concluded that one who constantly avoids and fears everything lacks courage, while one who recklessly confronts every danger lacks prudence. Courage is not the absence of fear – rather – it's about winning over our fears. Meaning that, you are brave because you conquer your fears, it's a thriving greatness in you, and it inspires greatness within others. In psychology, it's called Shock Therapy, and it suggests that if you constantly face your fears with courage, you train your brain to fire fewer fear signals in the *amygdala* and more in the *prefrontal cortex* – and if you forgot about it, it's the part responsible for logic and control. Do this repeatedly and you'll feel less fear and grow braver over time. It's neuroplasticity; your brain strengthens or weakens connections based on how often you use them. Fear doesn't control you. You rewire your brain. Face it. Trained it. Break it.

Building your feelings of self-worth is critical to overcoming your fears. Wanting something is not enough, you must hunger for it with your *inner roar,* and your motivation must be compelling to overcome the obstacles that will invariably come your way. Truth be told, you will face many defeats in life but never let yourself be defeated. You never fail until you stop trying. Always show up.

Fear does not have any special power unless you empower it by submitting it. As soon as you fear, you will suffer, meaning that you already suffered from your fears. Accept your fears and then move towards them because everyone overcoming their fears lives free.

Sure, there will be mistakes, expect critics, and it only means that you tried something new. Life has no limitations except the ones you make. I shared this earlier, but your mind will believe everything you will tell it because again, your thoughts are you and they are your cure and your *placebo. Darwin Theory* live within. So, when you fear and don't move on, you are not living with life, you are living in your mind. In life, everything you've ever wanted is on the other side of fear. To surpass and live with courage with your fears, my mentorship tip is as follows:

You can expose yourself to your deepest fear, the worst of all, and once you overcome it, no more fear has power, you are ready to beat the bullying effect it has on you every time it shows up. Once more, it's *Shock Therapy*. Another option is the following:

Slow progress is progress, face your fears one small, sweet pineapple bite at the time.

Many disturb themselves by imagining their whole life at once. If you spend too much time thinking about a thing, you'll never get it done. Make at least one definite move daily toward your goal like what is making one first step on the path building the path. To sit on an idea or fail to act on a goal is not really goal setting, but wishful thinking. Shoot at something, go beyond the limits of the Universe, that is where the stars are.

Again, there will be mistakes. A life spent making mistakes is not only more honorable, but more useful than a life spent doing nothing. Do not be embarrassed by your failures, learn from them, and start again. Every time you fail, you start again from a place of learning, and you also harvest commonality, inspiring people's hope with their future greatness. Do you remember about *the pratfall effect* from chapter 2?

Also, and again, expect critics. Many people in life are trapped in emotional illusions with *life & time*, and because they lack courage with themselves, they seek pleasure in taking others down with the thought it makes them feel better. That's the result of you doing something, saying something, and becoming someone. Truth be told, they wish they were you, and if they hate you, let them hate you because it means they are your biggest fan. It's life's *Law of Balance*. If you choose to live with the fear of failure, hardship, embarrassment, and let the negative voice of others take you down, you will never achieve your greatness.

Don't limit your challenges – rather – Challenge your limits. Without pushing your limits, without occasional risk, without occasional failures, you will never know what is truly possible in your life. If you can't do good crazy things from time-to-time, you're missing out with your living. Never forget that to become an expert with your passion, you must experience all possible mistakes, *be positively curious*, and a few of those mistakes will be harvested from an occasional risk.

I'm repeating myself and thank you for thinking of it because you are right, but often shared with my books, you will always harvest what you planted.

Remember that a beautiful day starts with a beautiful mindset, and you have control of your mindset. Feeling pain, fear, stress, anxiety about what you cannot control in life is a waste of your emotional energy, instead, *seek within* because you can control your inside, like using life's *Law of Balance* fundamental anchor.

What if you could turn a disadvantage into an advantage?
What if you could turn a liability into an asset?
What if a failure could become a success, and you turn your defeat into victory for clarity?

Fail, then Thrive

Frankfurt (DE) 2024 - Copyright Steve "Mr. Pineapple" Mathieu – Picture by Marc Maria

Sunday 13 Oktober 2024, cell phone in my right hand while I'm casually enjoying a walk in Old Frankfurt, and I was at the lookout for great captures and inspirational patterns. Because daily, everything surrounding us exhibit patterns speaking of life & leadership with analogies and metaphors when you observe them with open eyes and with an open mind. And when I saw a child fall off their 2-wheel bike, it sparked something in me.

At a young age, the process of riding a 2-wheel bike reminds us to move forward in life, and it's on a bumpy and challenging road requiring holding tight and keeping on moving while staying stable. Like a pineapple in balance.

Per a German proverb, all beginnings are hard.

We start riding a bike with 2 safety wheels and incrementally, a coach is removing one followed by the other. A basic process to build self-confidence with a new beginning and wire a new conditioned habit, and there were no magic beans. Assisted by a coach's encouragement, it's positive energy to build *positive affirmation* within oneself for future new beginnings.

In psychology, *positive affirmations* suggest a strategy to build self-esteem, boost confidence, and promote a positive outlook by challenging negative thoughts and behaviors, rooted in the self affirmation theory.

Another German proverb is failure makes smart.

Once both safety wheels are removed, the child is by themselves with someone shadowing. Like everything in life, new beginnings are hard because they are teamed with failures, and they can easily trouble one's ego and pride also reminding us to never let success reach our head and never let failure reach our heart.

When keeping focus on a goal, we achieve the goal because it was our focus. Meaning, the purpose of riding a 2-wheel bike like a pro and each fall becomes a lesson to improve a more solid foundation to keep balance while moving forward. The more challenging and uncomfortable, the more blooming and thriving the growth. You don't change the goal; you change your path to reach the goal. Like what is falling off the bike and getting back on: If you've failed, fixed, learned and did not repeat, you have not failed – rather - you have successfully risen.

Without an obsession for chasing inspiration, it often chases me instead, and what I witnessed that day inspires the following top 3 conclusions inspired by additional German proverbs.

Practice makes master.
In perspective, even when a master at something, master always keeps practicing and learning. The mindset you had to achieve what you have today, and if you don't improve it to your new reality, will be a mindset soon holding you back. Per my books, questions remain the same, but the answers are changing.

Good things take time.
Pineapple don't grow from magic beans. In an era for which everything is pressured with time, and for which it's easy to become overwhelmed, you are becoming someone you have never been before. Adjust to your daily new self and patience because you are becoming someone you have never been before.

If the rider is not good, it's the horse's fault.
Life is a do-it-yourself project, and building self-confidence from a solid foundation requires to *seek within*, not around. For everything that troubles you within from others, and from people's mistakes, you become an experienced bike rider when seeking within yourself to fix what troubles you and to learn from others' mistakes. Like a paperboy on their bike, no matter the weather and obstacles, keep riding your bike. My ride on my bike with a pineapple was in part, as follows.

When COVID-19 arrived in North America in 2019, I was announced a furlough status – meaning - a temporary layoff. I knew there was no way I would be called back to work. Not because I was not good at my job, but because it was a World crisis. An invisible threat that would not be eliminated easily. The following day after the announcement, I was updating my resume, researching for eLearning courses, and I started job hunting because per a rambling philosophy of The Pineapple Theory, ananas don't grow from magic beans. Don't sit and wait to be harvested because life is a do-it-yourself project, build your own path.

I was working in the airport environment, supporting a business in 15 airports spread out in Canada and the United States. Without work for ten months because of COVID-19, I looked back at my 20+ years of experience supporting the management of businesses. I have sought within from all angles. I applied my concept of the *sling shot principle* along with my concept of *coaching with the extreme obvious.*

The *sling shot principle* suggests pulling yourself back as much as you can until you touch your foundation, then observe the big picture before releasing yourself to go further, faster.

I realized that I felt crushed like a lemon by the *culture washing* of several corporate companies, by several *emotional fishermen*, and by how most of the society chooses to *think-act-speak* without ownership because the majority will be seeking around instead of within and the more extremes become slaves to their negative emotions. All become emotional illusions with *life & time* resulting in many losing themselves, forgetting themselves from the Myth and Mythology of their choosing resulting in many forgetting that they are, in life, positively the solution. I pulled way back with the *sling shot principle* and realized I was myself feeding what I identified to be a problem in the emotional illusions with *life & time.*

Prior to working in airports, I was 24 years old when promoted to a managerial position. My ambitions were at their prime and I was like a *baby pineapple.* Working in an unpleasant mix of a toxic corporate politic, I was often led without being provided any tools for personal growth. Feedback was often poorly shared and judgement without investigation ruled almost everyone. Perceptions were poorly managed; stress and pressure were terrible. Perfect definition of what corporate politic can be and become an environment becoming one. Yearly, layoffs were announced in my business unit because of never-ending restructures, and much more. I was not properly *fed,* and I made many, many mistakes. Often, I was unable to learn from or recover because of the toxic corporate politic environment.

Referred to as the *emotional spiderweb principle* in psychology, often experienced following a *Post Traumatic Shock Disorder (PTSD),* it's an analogy about our *semantic network* suggesting that key words from a souvenir will be stock on a subconscious spiderweb. When one or a combination of words are heard, the spiderweb shakes and all words become activated. Emotions from your souvenir are relived. Another psychological concept speaking similarly is Mood Congruent Memory, and here's its process:

The part of the brain responsible for memory is the *hippocampus*, but it doesn't work in isolation. It depends on cues to activate and filters what gets retrieved. Your brain has stored millions of memories from nearly every moment of your life, but you don't need all of them all the time. So, your mind filters certain cues that determine which memories are brought to the surface. One of the most powerful is processed by the *amygdala;* when you feel unfairly treated, the *amygdala*, sends this emotional signal to the *hippocampus*, which then activates that filter. It starts scanning your memory for events that fit that state. The selected memories reinforce your belief, intensifying the emotion, and creating a vicious cycle where emotion and memory constantly strengthen each other. This means that when emotions take over, what you are seeing is a filtered snapshot, not the full truth.

My *emotional spiderwebs* were full of negative souvenirs I've collected throughout my journey, and I became the negative souvenir of others. My *inner sweetness* was deeply hiding and held prisoner behind my *pineapple shell* because I did not know how to efficiently manage positively my emotions, and I wrongly used my *shell* which was more like a shield at the time. I did not know how to understand or manage biases and trusting others was challenging because of the corporate politic. Within was not balanced, there was a misalignment, several golden pieces within were covered, and I was seeking around instead of digging into myself.

Empathy – a valuable skill for one's inner sweetness – was clearly asleep in me and I come from a long way with this currency. Even today, like many people, I feel I'm always at risk of falling into my blind spot, especially when my *emotional batteries* have low energy. It is one of many reasons why those batteries must be recharged. Allow me to share an example.

The Golden Rule of empathy is known as: *Treating others as you want to be treated.* I have mentioned I come from a long way with empathy because I used to have the emotions of a rock. Therefore, the Golden Rule was not my friendly guide. When I was a child, I was left by myself with a life mindset of: Figure it out! Today, I'm relieved that my mistakes were not critical – within morality - and that I was able to positively lead myself. Figuring it out helped me to build a strong mind, become highly focus, seriously determinate, take initiatives and find my own solutions like an entrepreneur, stand up quickly when I fall, and more.

When I first experienced a leadership position, I was following the Golden Rule. I was comparing my employee's emotions with mine. I was listening to respond meaning I was looking at myself in their context instead of looking at them in their context *(Egocentric Theory)*. My empathy was not efficient because my *pineapple shell* was very thick like a shield, and my inner sweetness couldn't breathe.

When I heard about the Platinum Rule of empathy for the first time; *Do unto others as they would want to have done unto them*, it changed me like an idea activating a series of insightful thoughts. I had a tool to work with. It changed my perspective. I was able to positively improve myself and improve trust with my team. My inner sweetness started to breathe out more. Instead of comparing a member of my team's emotions with my personal bias emotions from where I come from - like looking at myself in a mirror - I started comparing them, with them. Meaning, seeing ones' emotions in the mirror when I was in front of it. I was listening to understand with *positive curiosity*.

One of the most used lines we say in the face of difficulties is the proverbial phrase, *when life gives you lemons, make lemonade*. The lemons in this phrase represent sourness or struggle while making lemonade means transforming lemons into something sweet or desirable. We have used this phrase so much that it has become a cliché, yet we still live in negativity.

When I saw life outside the emotional illusions with *life & time*, I sold my lemons and bought a pineapple! I progressively became me, Mr. Pineapple. My 3 faces became all connected to the same sweet roots; they became one. Life & leadership philosophies along with life principles were practiced and were acting like power tools to positively cultivate my roots and redefine my inner foundation keeping myself sweet within & around. Per life's *Law of Balance*, life is positive & negative forces complementing each other when in balance. A philosophy trackable since the 14th century B.C., and my pineapple became stable on my inner foundation, and my inner sweetness could breathe through my shell. It became my soul. A purpose took birth. Body – Mind – Soul. Though, this process can be painful, like an athlete training for the Olympics, and there are injuries; they're part of the journey's recipe. Here's a perspective about this summer and winter global event inspired by my travel to Athens in July 2022.

The Stadium - Athens (GR) 2022 – Copyright Steve "Mr. Pineapple" Mathieu - Photographer: Georgios Makkas

The stadium shown on the picture is where the first modern Olympics were held, in 1896, in Athens, Greece.

Toxic corporate politics in the workplace is in perspective, an extension of our history. Throughout Earth timeline, humans had the emotional need to be the best, and they still are. The need to become the best is an emotion, and emotions, they are built, and they have blind spots along with dark challenges because when one thinks for only themself, nothing good happens. *What was still is* throughout Earth timeline and many wanted to feel beyond being the best, they wanted to feel more powerful than several Gods society created and believe, using emotional negative actions which is still feeding society today:

- War.
- Suppressing humans' superpower to think for themselves and have them become followers.
- Creating a mindset of division and hate.
- Distorting truth for their own gain.
- And many more.

With in mind my purpose with The Pineapple Theory to cultivate pineHapply people by adding a pineapple to their life & leadership recipes, what if for humans to live more happily, together, requires them to be in competition with no one? What if humans had no desire to play a game of being better than anyone? What if each human was simply trying to become a better person than they were the day before, with themselves? In perspective, it's you who focus on your own lane because comparing yourself to others can be a deadly trap, and comparison is the thief of inner peace. It's a surefire way to destroy your focus, dilute your motivation, and distract you from your goals. Like the sharpest teeth that can't bite into water, the perspective serves to remind that your journey is unique, and your success is not measured by someone else's standards. Reading this book from the beginning, reflecting on the idea of people being in competition with no one, even myself don't see it happening. But can improvement be experienced like an athlete investing in themselves to become the best version of themselves?

- What if to become the best with yourself, you had to surround yourself with people that you consider better than you? *Darwin's Theory.*
- What if to become the best with yourself, you had to choose people that challenge and push you to succeed? *Positive affirmation.*
- What if to become the best with yourself, you had to always be a student? *Learn-to-Lean – Be positively curious.*
- Working backwards, what if to become the best with yourself, you first need to return to yourself, and know yourself? *The 5W's about you.*

One does not win the Olympics when things are easy. Olympics are won by facing challenges. Winning is not a miracle; it's the result of one's hard work. It's like in the absence of light; you become the light. One can only grow by facing challenges. Example: You wish to learn a new language, emerge yourself in a country speaking the language, alone. You'll need to speak it to survive. Becoming the best, like in sports, requires to be an action from a place a good within, and around.

What if every single person had to go through something that absolutely destroys them so they could figure out who they really are? The kind hearts have felt the most pain and I suggest being *positively curious* about their story, be inspired because you see, one day, you will also tell your story of how you overcame what you went through, and it will be someone else's survival guide that still moves societies from Myths & Mythologies. It will be your Olympic experience.

The Stadium in Delphi (GR) 2022 - Copyright and picture by Steve "Mr. Pineapple" Mathieu

It is said that every book you read better defines your soul because ones' writings is the geometry of their soul. As the guinea pig of my own theory, the idea of writing books came to mind and the ananas became my muse when the following happened, shared will all possible details in my title, *Worldwide fruitful travails with a pineapple.*

It was COVID-19's lockdown. I was sitting at my home desk, witnessing society's opposition to COVID-19 restrictions by acting like clowns and monkeys. There was a pineapple fruit viewed at a distance, and a big fruitful & sweet vision inspired me. It felt like a big bang, a flash from the future for which it speed was so fast, I hadn't seen the whole story. For reference purposes, it's like at the beginning of Marvel's movie - *Thor – Love & Thunder* – when the "wrong" picks up the *necro sword* and a flash of a purpose unfolds at the speed of light. To make a bowling reference, I could not see the goal to strike.

London (UK) 2025 - Copyright Steve "Mr. Pineapple" Mathieu – Picture by Hozir Sahdat

A valuable exercise for me when I have a vision is to see the math meaning that, when you can see it, you can better manage it. Like working with A.I.; you can't automate what you can't communicate. Therefore, I assembled a vision board. It's like a puzzle box I flip upside down and all the pieces are then assembled. Each piece of the puzzle represents a big vision or big idea. For The Pineapple Theory, it resulted in the following, and it became a mockup to engineer a first foundation, like the first plans to assemble Iron Man. Still today, when I think of something new, I refer to it because it was the original seed for thoughts making me a farmer.

Feed positively your roots - Master the art - Be inspired, be inspiring.

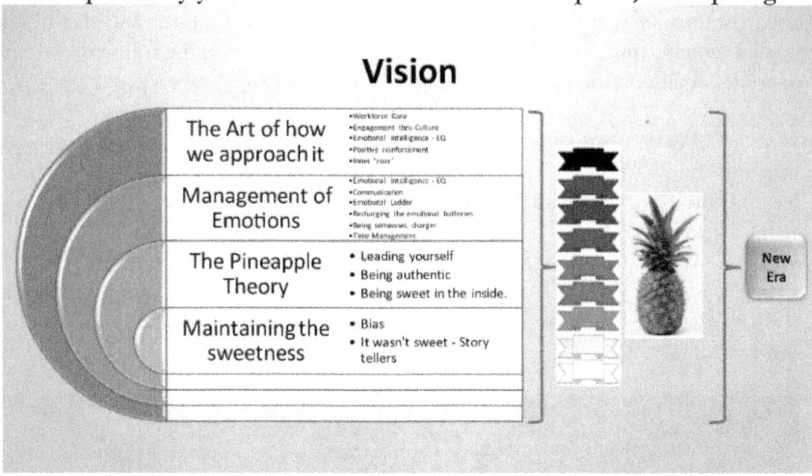

Original vision of The Pineapple Theory - Copyright by Steve "Mr. Pineapple" Mathieu

The first set of books I ever published are no longer available, in fact, some of them are viewed as collectables on eBay. They were as follows, and much of their content was included in this book's manuscript, and served to nurtured my theory.

When I unpublished them, my thought was to start fresh on new grounds because my understanding about my writing had grown. The following book was the first of the "2nd generation" and in 2025, I completely re-wrote the manuscript because my theory was officially completed. It resurrected in the 3rd generation, and it was the last and giving life to the *theoretical 3* fundamental anchor. Never 2 without 3 per a popular expression.

Mid-way between the 2nd and 3rd generation, the following titles were published and they are still available today. I've made final updates in 2025, but originally, they boosted my self-confidence with my research about our emotional patterns and how I can alternate how to speak about those patterns. In order of release:

The first title of the 3rd generation was my big project, *Worldwide fruitful travels with a pineapple,* being the one finally giving detailed responses about why anything & everything about the pineapple inspired to create pineapple analogies & metaphors to speak of life and humans with fruitful philosophy. The book is as authentic as the fruit looks, and it gave the most refreshing identity to The Pineapple Theory brand. Then, and here comes the big lesson, the *switcheroo.* Yes, Thrive, The Pineapple Theory, Feel & Think like a pineapple, and Reward yourself with the freedom of a pineapple, and Cultivte your seed for greatness books are almost the same, with their personalized variations, and simply presented with a different face meaning they have the same kind & sweet heart. In previous book editions, I continuously wrote that my books were like a big Lego set, and one day I told myself, *"Just f*** assemble it for them!"* I researched within my own research. The 3 books from the 3rd generation along with the *switcheroos* complete the cycle and my theory before moving to future projects and officially become the archetect of The Pineapple Theory. But wait because the confusion and compound of mistakes is not over because I've made, many mistakes.

It is said the first pancake is always a waste. Theoretically, I cannot share from whom or what might likely be the origin of this proverbial phrase, but often the first pancake is not as golden and slightly crispy as desired.

Like the old foundations under the Acropolis Museum, I would not say that the 1st and/or the 2nd generation of The Pineapple Theory were a waste – rather – they were inspirational pieces of jigsaw and fundamental seeds to cultivate a growth continuum of the pineapple, and myself. Daily, I have read several passages which inspired new text and travel projects giving me direction like a treasure map presented like a scavenger hunt, and I became the *guinea pig* of my own theory because the more I read, the more I experienced and practiced. It became the origin of the following quotation from my books: Even when a Master at something, Masters always keeps practicing and learning.

Previously shared, to become an expert, make all possible mistakes and sadly, I know, and I do not know, that I have not yet done them all. The learning from falling off my bike with a pineapple over again made my theory, the brand, and the messages matured & defined themselves because they were cultivated, they have grown, and the old foundation became the following imagery slogan reminding me, and for the readers who have followed my work because they believe about it since the beginning, to always look from where you came from when you think you don't make progress.

Copyright by Steve "Mr. Pineapple" Mathieu

A bad start isn't a bad finish and when you have failed, engrave the following in your temple:

FAIL: First Attempt In Learning.
END: Effort Never Dies.
And when you're told, NO, remember; it's your Next Opportunity.

That's how you thrive. That's how you wear the crown. It's Ethics of Persistence because "No" builds you, not breaks you.

Rejection isn't the end; it's redirection. Every "No" is a signal, not of failure, but of refinement. Each closed door teaches you something: about timing, about resilience, about adjusting your approach.

This is the essence of *Practice Theory*: growth through repetition. The more you expose yourself to rejection, the less power it holds. This is *Desensitization* in action, not emotional numbness, but emotional strength. You learn to separate your worth from the outcome. You stop flinching at "No" and start learning from it.

But repetition alone isn't enough. *Deliberate Practice Theory* (Ericsson et al., 1993) reminds us that progress comes not from quantity alone, but from intentional refinement. Every "No" is feedback. It tells you: this version wasn't quite right. Not yet. Keep going. Keep improving. Because the goal isn't just to hear "Yes", it's to become someone worthy of it.

This is where philosophy and psychology converge.

Seneca wrote, *"A gem cannot be polished without friction, nor a man perfected without trials."* Rejection is friction. It sharpens, not shatters.

Nietzsche said, *"He who has a why to live can bear almost any how."* The "why" gives rejection its purpose. Without it, persistence becomes aimless.

And in *The Pineapple Theory*, we expand the "why" through *Be Positively Curious.* This principle invites us to approach setbacks with warmth and wonder. It's the first thought, voice, and action that leads to uncovering deeper purpose. Curiosity, when paired with respect, turns resistance into insight.

Psychologically, this is about *Construal Level Theory* (Trope & Liberman, 2010). "No" thinkers operate in low-level construal; focused on immediate obstacles. "Yes" thinkers operate in high-level construal; focused on long-term meaning. It also ties to *Growth Mindset* (Dweck, 2006): rejection isn't a verdict; it's feedback. Those with a growth mindset see "No" as a signal to adapt, not retreat.

But here's the line that must never be crossed:

This mindset is about growth, not pressure. It's about perseverance, not pursuit. Never apply this philosophy in situations where "No" means stop. Respect is not negotiable. Boundaries are not steppingstones. Persistence must never become entitlement. The right "Yes" will never require you to ignore someone else's "No."

Practice Exercises: Ethical Resilience

1. **Rejection Journal**
   Track each "No" you receive this week. Note what you learned, how you responded, and what shifted in your mindset.
2. **Boundary Audit**
   Reflect on one moment where persistence may have crossed into pressure. What would ethical perseverance have looked like instead?
3. **Deliberate Refinement**
   Choose one area where you've received repeated "No." Break it down. What specific skill, behavior, or approach needs improvement?
4. **Curiosity Practice**
   When faced with resistance, ask: "What can I learn from this?" Write down three insights. Let curiosity lead your next move.
5. **Reframe Ritual**
   Each time you hear "No," say aloud: "This is not rejection—it's redirection." Let it become a mantra.

Thankfulness

Sad to say, but many people will notice and point out the one mistake you made, no matter how many successful resolutions you've made before. Without thought, a negative emotion is given a free fast track to their inner sweetness, inside/out. Like if thinking differently was too much effort or not worth their time in the emotional illusions with *life & time.*

Their voice or text feels like a slap to one's face because they are often the only ones speaking, while recognition is often kept silent, and *soooooory*, but silent recognition is no recognition. If we make an application of the *egocentric theory,* the slap to the face is like a child stopping everything they do, running to you all excitedly to share something negative about you. Then, the child runs away. Yes, the child stopped everything and felt a sense of urgency to share something negative about you, and it made them falsely happy. Simply standing, you just received a free cheap slap to the face!

With my title, *Market & Sell yourself, products, services like a pineapple,* backed by data, I suggest the perspective about the pattern about 1%-3% standard of people will emotionally act impulsively, and this easily can influence a large movement of undecided people giving value to *social proof.*

In psychology, *social proof* suggests that people often copy the actions and opinions of others, especially when unsure of the "right" way to behave, as they assume others possess more knowledge or insight about a situation. And opinions from *social proof* easily become your *Superego* because of the *mere exposure effect.* Here's why:

You don't choose how you see the world. Your worldview isn't original. It was programmed into you, and now you defend beliefs you never consciously chose. The human brain is not designed for independent thought in the way most people imagine, and with The Pineapple Theory, I wish to break this pattern. Roughly 90–95% of cognitive activity happens subconsciously (Bargh & Morsella, 2008). This means your so-called "opinions" are often nothing more than reflections of repeated exposure. Your subconscious doesn't argue, it absorbs. Every social media post, every headline you skim, every slogan you hear becomes part of the mental code you operate on, often without awareness.

That's the *mere exposure effect* (Zajonc, 1968). Your brain equates repetition with truth. That's why common narratives, even false or extreme ones, become internalized over time. If you're repeatedly fed messages like "people are selfish" or "the system is broken," those phrases will start to feel true, not because you've reasoned through them, but because your brain has heard them enough.

This creates an illusion of agency. You believe you're making choices, when in reality you're just executing scripts written by others. From family conditioning to media saturation, your identity is shaped by what you consume, not what you consciously choose. Trash in; trash out.

This isn't conspiracy theory, it's cognitive science. You will always be influenced. The question is not if, but by whom. If your inputs are dominated by negativity, hopelessness or resentment, those patterns will define your internal world. But if you surround yourself with models of strength, clarity and constructive action, your subconscious adopts those patterns instead. It's *Darwin's Theory.*

Your brain is programmable. Every input writes a line of code. Being *positively curious* is a solution for clarity and being the *guinea pig* harvest your truest opinion.

Apple's new product release is an *extreme obvious* about the suggested 1%-3% standard. Think about it, with 8 billion humans on this planet, there are a few who will camp for a week only to become a first-time user. Then, their opinion about the new product builds a path for *social proof.* Season 8 of The Office adapted the Apple reality with humor with the launch of the Pyramid device.

I'm conducting an ongoing experiment with social media using my *Master File-Journal-Communicate principle.* Still today I journal data for each social media post I have released since 2022. With more than 5,000 posts in my Master File, it confirms that only 1%-3% of viewers of a post versus the post impression engage with a post. Brutal right? Per the Lean Six Sigma Methodology, there are random results outside the standard deviation. But like Thanos in The Avengers -The Infinity Stones, *"All this effort for a little drop of blood."*

Amazon's book reviews are the same and an impactful example. Myself, with my books, I'm no exception and can't escape the 1%-3% of harsh feedback, although, I always find interesting that the loud voices giving a slap to the face are hiding who they are but people who have great things to share will not hide. About Amazon's 1%-3% book reviews, for example, I researched for international best sellers, authors who sold millions of copies of their work and the following is a tiny sample of people's impulsive emotional feedback without recognizing the hundreds of things they liked.

1-Star rating because the book had been received slightly damaged when delivered by Amazon.

1-Star rating because the reader prefers hearing the author speak and no one should read the book.

1-Star rating because of a handful of typos.

Lastly from many other examples, when setting a paid marking with META, the built-in math projection also gives 1%-3% engagement or click from your paid impressions.

If you have someone in your surrounding part of the 1%-3% standard, the following thought influencing approach can help you thrive to influence a behavioral change, and it is referred to as *negative identity framing effect.*

In psychology, *negative identity framing effect* suggest that people tend to prefer a certain option when the decision is framed positively ("you will win $100" vs. "you have a chance of winning $200") but prefer the risky option when the decision is framed negatively ("you will lose $100" vs. "you have a chance of losing $200"). Alternatively, it's an unwanted action to trade people's fears and they'll avoid it at all costs. Let's make application of it as follows.

While talking casually, you could say, *"Hey Pina, you know what I really respect about you? When one thing makes you feel negative, you seek for everything you've liked about it first, and I truly admire that."*

Let that seed for thought sink in, then moments later, bring up someone else. *"You know, not like Pomodoro though, who consistently with impulsivity will be lead with negativity and be blind to everything they liked."*

The brain now links being silent about what they liked first with being negative and not being admired for which conflicts with the identity you've given them earlier. They accepted an identity because it validated them (Ego and selfishness fundamental anchor). This creates *cognitive dissonance* acting against their own beliefs or identity feels uncomfortable.

In psychology, *cognitive dissonance* suggests that people experience discomfort when their actions or beliefs conflict with their values, leading them to seek ways to reduce this tension, often by changing their beliefs or behaviors to achieve consistency.

Controlling our emotions by engaging in our mind with the purpose of recognizing the good first is nothing new with our timeline, and a sample of emotional patterns gives value to wise voices to educate more awareness with gratefulness.

Albert Einstein
The best way to cheer yourself is to cheer somebody else up.

Dalai Lama
When you practice gratefulness, there is a sense of respect toward others.

Bruce Lee
Real living is living for others.

Richard Branson
They encouraged me to always look for good in people instead of assuming the worst and trying to find fault.

Like anger and for everything negative, when you don't act, you wire your brain at becoming stronger at thriving with positiveness. Before expressing uncontrolled negative emotions, use your mind and ask yourself; what are the hundreds of things I liked and have not recognized?

Thrive by recognizing 99% of what you've like instead of the 1% of dislike, like in a pineapple plantation; if one ananas out of 100 is "defect", have you acknowledged the remaining 99 tasteful good ones?

Like comparison being the thieves of inner peace, envy is the thieves of thankfulness. Everything you hate about others is a mirror to our own self. Psychology calls it *projection*. And there are ways to break free, take control and ownership of ourselves, and humbly wear the pineapple crown stable with self-awareness. Here's a series of perspectives:

Every time someone else gets praise - recognition, or success - you smile politely, but internally, you feel like it should have been you. That's not insecurity. It's biology.

What you're experiencing is called *status motivation*, a deeply embedded evolutionary drive. Human beings are social mammals, and throughout evolutionary history, status meant access to resources, protection and mating opportunities (Henrich & Gil-White, 2001). As a result, your brain is hardwired to constantly track social hierarchies, even if you're not consciously aware of it.

This means that in every interaction, your mind runs an internal algorithm: Where do I stand? The moment someone rises, through praise - visibility or achievement -

your relative position feels threatened. Not because you're weak, but because your brain interprets their success as a potential risk to your standing. This often triggers envy, which research shows is a natural emotional response to upward social comparison (van de Ven et al., 2009).

Most people try to repress this feeling, they pretend it doesn't exist, hide it behind fake support, or mentally discredit the other person's success. It becomes their *Shadow Self.* But repression only makes things worse. Unacknowledged status drives often rot to bitterness, resentment and passive sabotage. The paradox is that a person who hates another becomes their biggest fan. Admiration is passive. Envy is active. It keeps people watching, hoping they'll fall. And every view, every whisper, every prayer for failure adds fuel. If someone you hate never falls, they'll turn spite into power. The more you resent, the more the other rise, and the more you spread their name. Once more, it's the *Law of Balance.* and it's influenced by a phenomenon called *Schadenfreude.*

Its psychological roots lie deep. In *social comparison theory* (Festinger, 1954) and dominance hierarchies encoded by evolution. When someone in your perceived rank fails publicly, the drop reshuffles your position upward without any effort on your part. That's why the brain rewards it with dopamine: it's an ego boost disguised as moral outrage. Neuroscience confirms this. fMRI studies (e.g. Takahashi et al., 2009) show that observing the misfortune of envied individuals activates reward centers in the brain, the same areas triggered by food, sex, or winning. It's not morality that governs reactions. It's rank, threat, and relief.

There is a better path. Channel the drive instead of denying it. Pick a domain, training, business, art, anything and make it your competitive arena. In psychology, this is called *sublimation* (Freud, 1914): redirecting raw drives into socially constructive outlets. In this case, instead of envying other people's progress, you use it as fuel to outgrow your current self. Like being a wolf hungrier than the wolf you view at the top of the mountain.

If you don't give your status hunger a goal, it becomes toxic. But if you give it structure and direction, it turns into ambition. The difference between envy and excellence is what you do with discomfort.

Then, sublimated envy; *The Underdog Effect.* This social psychology shows that people root for the underdog not because of empathy, but because it gives them permission to project their own resentment onto those in power. This is fueled by status frustration (Veblen, 1899; Bourdieu, 1977) and deep-seated relative deprivation, the psychological discomfort of feeling powerless while others rise.

When someone challenges authority, it creates a projection surface: the challenger becomes a vessel for our suppressed frustrations, while the powerful become symbols of everything we've been denied status, control, recognition. Studies (Kim et al., 2008) show that people consistently support underdogs in asymmetrical conflicts, especially when they feel the system is rigged. But this support is conditional, it's not about justice, it's about vengeance by proxy.

Strategically, this means if you want mass support, don't appear dominant. Appear defiant. Make people feel you weren't supposed to win. That narrative gives them an emotional outlet and gives you their loyalty, not because they love you, but because you help them hate safely. Here's a guinea pig experiment about this from my Authorship journey.

Every year at the Frankfurt Book Fair, I exhibit with purpose. My small & charming, 2x2 meter stand - colorful, alive, and fruitfully breathing The Pineapple Theory - faces the towering landmark of HarperCollins Publishers. It's no coincidence, I have fairs organizers for this location, and I disguise experiments. And every year, I witness a pattern.

Visitors walk by filming and photographing only the HarperCollins sign. As if that's the highlight of their fair visit. Even a government official, flanked by bodyguards, paused only to capture the sign, completely ignoring the stand beside it. This is not malice. It's blindness. It's the conditioned behavior that keeps people trapped in scripted narratives, missing the sweetness that stands quietly beside them. The underdog. This is how small entrepreneurs die when their offerings from the heart go unseen. And it goes deeper.

When I witness people throwing themselves at the giants' boxed offerings - without even consulting what they're purchasing in bulk - it reveals the shape of their comfort zone. It's not curiosity. It's compliance. And for the 1–3% of offerings that dare to step outside the standard, the blind dissonance makes people uncomfortable. It makes them weak. Because it challenges the script. And that's where my work comes in. That's exactly what my books speak about - in part.

- To disturb the standard with authenticity.
- To awaken emotional clarity.
- To offer fruitfulness beside the commercial box.

But here's the truth:

It takes more than motivation to stand tall and fruitful like a pineapple in front of these giants. It takes consistency. It takes emotional strength. It takes a commitment to keep alive what deserves to live outside the standard, and to inspire others to build their own history. Because history isn't made by those who follow the signs. It's made by those who notice what's beside them. And sometimes, the most meaningful stories are the ones that weren't expected but were always there.

When I exhibited at the 2025 Frankfurt Bookfair, my book inventory sold out at midday on Saturday, 2nd day of fair with the general public. Along with several sweet psychological techniques to get their attention and informed them: The Pineapple Theory is an underdog. And among several more fruitful ingredients, I also said: It's imperfectly perfect. Here's why:

It's the *Arch of Tactical Misdirection.* Because people love finding flaws, and when to find one, they feel clever about pointing it out and stop looking for anything else. They stop digging deeper. That's when 1-star ratings are recorded for nonsense. To counter that, I create my own flaw, and they looks real enough to attack, but fake enough not to hurt. Then, they think they understand me better.

The fruit is beside you. Not behind the sign. Ignore it, and you become the weapon of the killer.

Thankfulness isn't just a virtue—it's a vision. And when you choose to recognize the sweetness beside the sign, you don't just thrive. You lead. You wear the crown with purpose.

Overthinking

Overthinking isn't a character flaw, it's a cognitive response rooted in *Intolerance of Uncertainty* (IU), a psychological construct that describes how strongly someone reacts to ambiguous or unpredictable situations. Research by Dugas et al. (1998) shows that individuals high in IU interpret uncertainty as inherently stressful, which leads to excessive worry and mental rehearsal of worst-case outcomes.

Neurobiologically, this state is maintained by persistent activation in the *orbitofrontal cortex* (OFC), the brain region responsible for evaluating potential risks. Without a clear outcome, the OFC keeps scanning for resolution, which never arrives without action. This creates a cognitive feedback loop: more thinking leads to more uncertainty, not clarity.

The therapeutic solution lies in behavioral experimentation, a core method in *Cognitive Behavioral Therapy* (CBT). According to Bennett-Levy et al. (2004), deliberately engaging in small, uncertain actions generates prediction error, a mismatch between feared outcomes and reality. This disrupts the loop and forces the brain to update its beliefs about uncertainty and danger. Picture this classic: It the water cold or hot? You start small by dipping the tip of a toe.

By documenting your fear, the action you took, and the real result, you externalize the experience and create retrievable proof that uncertainty is survivable. This reduces the brain's need to over-simulate, gradually building cognitive tolerance for ambiguity.

Now, per The Pineapple Theory's philosophical lens, if you keep everything within, with time, it will give power to negativity. Thinking back about the wisdom of several Myths & Mythologies from our timeline, people are encouraged to confess what troubles them, and their "sins". Everything exiting you loses power, and I can only share the following *extreme obvious* awareness; disturbing society by blocking a bridge at peak hour or access to an international airport for what troubles you is too much.

In my journal of inspiration, I have a handful of clever analogies being insightful cues with the purpose to inspire clarity with your overthinking and feel less overwhelmed.

The Flamingo Theory

Kowloon Park, Hong Kong 2025 - Copyright and picture by Steve "Mr. Pineapple" Mathieu

When feeling crushed by life and by your own thoughts, remember to *seek within* because in the emotional illusions with *life & time*, your fundamental anchors are your power tools assisting you at becoming a problem solver. Make time to pause and gently structure your thoughts in your mind because, again, your mind is your temple.

Throughout Earth timeline, life requires keeping balance with opposite forces, a philosophy from the 14th century B.C. and in perspective, can you keep balance like a Flamingo standing tall on one leg?

If you struggle at keeping balance in the emotional illusions with *life & time* because there are thoughts within, or people around, acting like Ace Ventura shooting paper balls at you (Referred to the movie Ace Ventura, When Nature Calls), remember that you are not alone. Being with others is **flamboyance!** Connect with someone to voice your inner battles or journal them because it's your soul speaking on paper. Think of someone who can be emotionally & thoughtfully rational to assist you at being *positively curious* within because it will assist you to return to your true self because again, when we voice the negative, the negative becomes less powerful.

To know where to go, you first need to know where you're at. Don't wait for life to change you because life is the one waiting for you to change. Never lose yourself, never forget yourself in the emotional illusions with *life & time.* If you wonder what pineapple has in common with a Flamingo, other than both being an exotic match,

Flamingos are pink because of what they eat, and The Pineapple Theory is positive nutriments & vitamins for one's inner sweetness and thoughts. In other words, in life, you become what you consume which is an interpretation of *Darwin's Theory*. Positively feed your roots to become more positive within, leading to becoming more positive around because you will always attract from who you are within.

Las Vegas 2022 - Copyright and picture by Steve "Mr. Pineapple" Mathieu

The Sunflower Theory

Not only does pineapples inspires my analogies & metaphors, but a sunflower also can speak of life & humans.

With my careful observation at detecting emotional patterns with tens of thousands of years with our timeline, humans were taught that the positive is Up, meaning, look up! Must I add, in marketing, luxury brands use this knowledge by showing you with a big close-up of their product looking down at you, pushing you to look up.

The *Up concept* is simple; it's where the light and good energy is, and our ancestors understood that a very long time ago by writing this concept and philosophy into their manuscripts.

A sunflower looks at the sun, follows it, grows from it and it blooms and grows fast. Because of life's *Law of Balance*, it's not always sunny. Meaning, expect clouds from time-to-time along with rain to clean up and water your soil becoming a place of learning from self-reflection. No thunder needed though because only rain makes something grow.

The beauty of nature and inspiring *The Sunflower Theory* is this; when there's no light/sun, sunflowers turn to each other, they face each other to share their good energy and light.

This information builds an insightful bridge about the Peace & Love movement from the 70s because the flower was symbol for more Peace when chaos was disturbing Freedom, also explaining why I suggest cultivating indoor plants. Cultivate to bloom.

In life, when there are clouds, speaking to someone positive with wise thoughts is absorbing their positivity to recharge because the sun can always be found above the clouds. Recharging our *emotional batteries* can be done thanks to someone else's energy. It's human medicine.

Unclog your mind

There are several reasons why your Mind is Full, meaning overwhelmed, and it's often from several activated thoughts at the same time leading your emotions into a tight funnel. When I coach, it always amazes me how being overwhelmed follows the emotional pattern of people's top 3 disrupters of their good vibe and happiness of the day.

When feeling overwhelmed, I suggest the following top 3 servings of servings of pineapple-inspired clarity as simple action items and written exercises to structure yourself because it's a journal activity, and when Mindful, you take full control of yourself, you de-escalate the overwhelming feeling by giving clarity to your thinking because a calm mind sees things with clarity:

- (1) Give your *emotional batteries* a positive boost with your *daily emotional booster*. A common pattern is when overwhelmed and feeling crushed by negativity, people leave this important process aside first when in fact, it's the first needed thing and most important because you must charge yourself with what makes you feel happier to remove misery. It's life *Law of Balance,* always bring balance back. A rested mind always comes back more focused, sharper, and stronger.
- (2) Declutter your space for mental clarity. It serves as a reminder to always focus on what you can control because what you can control makes life easier. In your control, your words, thoughts, response, actions, self-awareness, and how you treat others.
- (3) Write down what you need to get done and focus on one task at a time based on importance. It's like eating a pineapple, eat it one small, sweet bite at a time. Make the best of the time management tools shared in this book. When completing tasks on your list, put a "checkmark", it will energize your primitive behavior of *motion* and nurture a visual of accomplishment.

In psychology, the behavioral primitive of *motion* refers to fundamental, automatic, and involuntary movement patterns that are considered building blocks of more complex actions. These primitives, like reflexes, are often linked to survival and basic needs, and their continued presence or influence in later life can impact motor skills, cognitive abilities, and even mental well being.

My top 3 recommendations have not been invited from imagination. They are harvested from neuroscience with a concept called *Cognitive Load Theory* (CLT) developed by John Sweller (1988), and it explains why mental overload kills productivity, and it's not laziness. It's explained by your working memory, the brain's mental scratchpad, has very limited capacity. Older research (Miller, 1956) estimated 7±2 chunks, but modern studies (Cowan, 2001) reduce this to just 4 items. When this system is overloaded, performance crashes: you procrastinate, forget tasks, and lose focus.

CLT distinguishes three types of loads:

1. Intrinsic load – the complexity of the task itself.
2. Extraneous load – distractions, multitasking, unnecessary decisions.
3. Germane load – mental effort spent forming useful knowledge structures.

Your goal is to reduce extraneous load, manage intrinsic load, and maximize germane load. *Sooooory*, but as advertised earlier in this book, the following will be coaching variants always shared. Practical neuroscience strategies:

- Externalize information (to-do lists, planning tools). According to the *Extended Mind Theory* (Clark & Chalmers, 1998), the brain offloads information to the environment, treating external tools as cognitive extensions.
- Break down tasks. Don't "write a report", write the title, then the intro. This reduces intrinsic load and prevents mental paralysis. It's the frame of a jigsaw.

- Use the *Pomodoro Technique,* developed by Francesco Cirillo. It structures work into 25-minute focus blocks with short breaks. Research (Bailey & Konstan, 2006) shows timeboxing enhances focus and reduces task aversion. It leverages *Temporal Motivation Theory* (Steel & König, 2006), which explains that proximity of reward increases motivation.
- Design your environment. Eliminate digital noise, automate trivial decisions (e.g., outfit choice), and batch similar tasks. High performers across domains do exactly this to preserve cognitive energy for what matters.
- Neuroscientific evidence (D'Esposito & Postle, 2015) shows that reducing competing cognitive demands leads to better activation in the prefrontal cortex, the area responsible for planning and executive control.

<u>The Las Vegas Theory</u>

With 8 billion people on our planet living with their emotions differently means that our self-control is consistently tested and under pressure. Our strength is not only about keeping ourselves in control and balance with what surrounds us, in fact, the battlefield is more intense within ourselves because that's where it all starts. Though, with the purpose at keeping our *emotional batteries* healthy, time comes to let ourselves go crazy because it's the *Law of Balance.* It's like someone on a strict diet, they will need a cheat meal from time-to-time because if not, the day there's a leak with what they worked hard to control will brutally become out of control. The 2004 movie Dodgeball gives viewers a funny perspective at the end about a consequence of losing control with our cravings. Similarly, when our mind overthinks, a good break with the purpose to recharge and give a break to our conscious thinking gives light to our non-conscious. On our wicked planet, there's one place that inspired other countries at having something similar, Las Vegas.

Throughout Earth timeline, several Myths & Mythologies took birth and still lives today. Myths & Mythologies sharing perspectives to understand life and humans emotionally better. Remove the illusions of their storytelling and their raw concept can be seen. Their raw concept is their purpose: Assist humans to live happily, together. To live happily together starts within each one of us because when we experience positive emotions, we become positive with others, and it's referred to as *Ideomotor theory* in psychology.

What was from the 14th century B.C. *still is*: Positive & Negative forces, opposites forces complementing each other when in balance. Tell a human not to do something and the human will likely do the opposite which is referred to as *reactance* in psychology. Dark emotional challenges such as alcohol, drugs, gambling, money, and sexuality are some examples of what several Mythologies throughout Earth timeline refer as the bad, from the Devil, are Sin because they are addictive pleasures, not happiness. To either suppress their need or control them to ensure that one does not lose and forget themselves requires emotional energy from their inner sweetness, and pineapple shell. Because humans' emotions are peculiar, sometimes, what is negative is needed inside our pineapple shell to recharge our positive energy. This perspective is explored with Marvel's 2016 movie Dr. Strange, when the *Sorcerer Supreme* requires sourcing – from time-to-time - strength from the negative and per The Pineapple

Theory, I suggest escaping reality inside reality!

What happens in Vegas stays in Vegas is a powerful quotation for what is now known as SIN CITY. A place designed to escape reality and be surrounded by the "negative" cultivating what is positive. A place surrounded with an inclusion of diversity, from those who gives the perception they did not pack clothes to consume alcohol each hour on the clock. A place where hands down, everyone wishes to have fun and feel like the rules of life are on break for the duration of their visit. Many will exhibit freedom of their happiness when walking and feeling stressed free from *life & time.* Because life requires opposites, it's obvious there are always a few people stretching this concept too much, becoming unpleasant.

In perspective, Las Vegas can be viewed as a real-life training room for one's fundamental anchors. Escaping reality requires *emotional energy* with the purpose of recharging with the fun of what is "negative" because one's life principles still must be applied to keep it reality. If not, one can easily lose & forget themself. Example: Gambling in Las Vegas is only fun when you can block the dark emotional challenges of gambling with your pineapple shell. Therefore, keep what should be fun...fun within & around when escaping reality inside reality.

As humans, we all need to recharge our *emotional batteries* and there are several ways to do it. SIN CITY is one of them, needed from time to time allowing humans to escape the problems of reality with their mind. Even in most hotels, the Bible is not available with the purpose of truly allowing people to break free. For me, September 2022 was my fourth experience and not the last. In fact, what was the purpose of giving my mind a break turned out to become a blooming 4 days of inspiration, and when escaping reality within reality, one thing must never change in life: Be kind, be respectful, have good manners, and never – ever – harm.

If you feel the need to recharge your *emotional batteries* differently and give a break from overthinking, escaping reality inside reality is a working solution and good news, you are one flight ticket away which will make you say: "Vegas baby!"

Las Vegas 2022 - Copyright and picture by Steve "Mr. Pineapple" Mathieu

Proactive over reactive

Post-COVID-19 in Canada, worst in Montreal, was experienced chaos with the passport renewal process. The masses reacted with their emotional desire to travel, increasing demand, and breaking the workload. Endless queues at passport offices for which people had to miss work. Although delays were largely covered by the media, a few would still attend the queue without bringing snacks and water and later faint, blaming everything except their lack of preparedness. During COVID-19, truer when the masses were on lockdown, plenty of time was available to proactively keep themselves busy at updating everything "administrative" in their life, including having an up-to-date passport. For many, complaining was their priority.

On the other hand, emotional patterns from our timeline dictates that society is reactive to their needs, the online purchase culture amplified this behavior, and this requires businesses and public services to act proactively before pain forces itself like an unwelcome guest, also known as Risk Management and Readiness. Life's *Law of Balance* was experienced, and long-term solutions were forced to be created and released for which today, the process is updated, smoother, but will require to always be kept solid to remain solid when there's extra weight on the foundation if there's learning from history.

With my title, *Market & Sell yourself, products, services like a pineapple,* I shared the following perspective speaking of humans being reactive over proactive for which, we must respond by giving Love – Time – Health by relieving a pain, saving a fear, and realistically support ambitions & hopes.

"Sadly, many are waiting for life to force them to change when life is the one waiting for them to change. They will share excuses such as, they don't have the budget, now is not the time or it's not their priority, or they don't need it. I once heard the following and found it inspiring; if you truly do not wish to spend, why are you stepping inside a shopping mall?

When there's pain, psychologically, their emotions dominate and become their emotional illusion with life & time, meaning that their emotions are no longer bridged with their rationale. Here's an example:

One could proactively purchase an air conditioner for their residence, but they don't need it for now because the temperature is comfortable, or they don't have the budget for it, or they don't have the time for it. Until a heat wave hits, and they have not slept for 3 nights. Because there's pain, their emotions take over and magically, there's time and money."

Humans' tendency to procrastinate is an emotional pattern that can't hide with our timeline. The masses *was and still is* more reactive rather than proactive. From washing their hands, coughing in their elbow, and wearing a face mask when sick to prevent the spread of any form of viruses to not text-and-drive, don't drink and drive, and many...many more. The majority demonstrate the need to experience negativity from an event affecting them emotionally. For a smaller portion, an event that will absolutely destroy them, becoming an illness forced to be taken care of. It's like a child told not to touch fire *(loss aversion* "meeting" with *reactance),* and they still do. A wise voice had spoken and yet, it was not listened, only the *guinea pig* experience was a teacher. Here's the face of psychology about this with coaching solutions:

Procrastination is not a time management issue. It's an emotion regulation problem. When you say, "I'll do it later," what your brain is really doing is avoiding discomfort and that avoidance is neurologically reinforced through negative reinforcement. You remove the uncomfortable task, and your brain rewards you with relief. That short-term relief becomes addictive.

At the core is a cognitive bias called *Temporal Discounting* (Ainslie, 1975). The brain heavily devalues rewards the further they are in the future. So long-term goals - like building a career, mastering a skill, fixing your health updating a passport - feel less urgent than short-term pleasures like scrolling, snacking or for many, complaining. Positively, you're not lazy. Your *prefrontal cortex*, responsible for planning and impulse control, is constantly in conflict with your *limbic system,* which demands instant gratification.

Compounding this is *status quo bias* and the illusion of readiness. Your nervous system equates change with threat, triggering the *amygdala's* fear response. That's why even thinking about starting something important can make you feel tired, anxious, or "not ready." Readiness, however, is not a state, it's a side effect of action. When people say "they were lucky" – *sooooory* – but they were ready. Waiting to feel ready is just disguised fear.

Mental contrasting and implementation intentions (Oettingen & Gollwitzer, 2001) act as a solution.
First, identify what you're avoiding.
Then force your brain to confront the cost of inaction. That triggers the *insular* (emotion bodily state integration) and increases urgency.
Pair this with a specific, non-negotiable action: one uncomfortable step daily before comfortable activities. Action before avoidance. Movement before mood.

You don't need more time. You need fewer lies. And the lie that matters most is that your future self will somehow be braver than you are now. And *soooooory,* but it won't.

Let's keep exploring this topic from The Pineapple Theory's philosophical len.

Proactive mindset
Like how you choose to live your life and the pineapple you select at the market, a proactive mindset is a choice and freedom available for everyone. Sadly, because there's no emotional perfection, a portion of society will be slave to their negative emotions which troubles the purpose for humans to live more happily together. The patterns from our history demonstrate this knowledge about humans' emotions is well known since tens of thousands of years and books of rules along with consequences were needed for nearly everything with the purpose of influencing balance with positive & negative forces. Freedom is often over stretched for which many will do things for themselves until controls are imposed to provide balance. What if freedom was misunderstood or what if people do not know how to live with it?

Reactive society
With a proactive mindset, society has the freedom to do the right things to greatly assist the right things to happen to them. This view becomes extremely important when understood by top leaders and per The Pineapple Theory, in life, everyone is already the top leader. Sadly, this freedom is pushed to the extreme by the negative being the trigger of events forcing society to become reactive. Hospitals, Prisons, and Graveyards are suggested being the top 3 locations to understand life. Though, the ultimate outcome for one's reaction at teaching proactivity from their new mindset is from the passing of someone they loved.

Society by influence
Every human for a total of 8 billion of them have the freedom to do the right things for the right things to happen to them. Another pattern from our timeline is the masses in need to consistently be influenced to do the right things. Sadly, something

will be supported by the majority only if it is popular, and this escalates with *meme theory*.

In psychology, *meme theory* explains the development of culture through the imitation of things: ideas, behaviors, and styles that are encoded as memes so they can be easily imitated. To speak your inner child; monkey sees, monkey do.

Humans' emotions are peculiar, and it's a calling to thrive with our mind. What is wrong will be encouraged without being challenged by the majority and become popular while what is right but not popular will be ignored and must be influenced. It's exhausting for everyone with an understanding about what is right & wrong in the emotional illusions with *life & time,* from a place of good for others. Eventually, the majority will hang their head in shame when they realize the wrong, they defended & encouraged, and the right they've ridiculed.

For a remaining portion, eventually, the right things are imposed leading the majority to become reactive. Onced impose, many will seek around instead of *seeking within.* If the majority would seek within, they would realize they had the ability to do the right things all along, by themselves. It's like one driving their vehicle alone, they choose to drive 60km/hr + over the speed limit. They get caught by a police officer and must pay a fine forcing them to follow the speed limit for their safety, and others. Many being the receiver of the fine will seek around instead of within. Furthermore, a smaller portion of the receivers of a fine will seek around on social media to cultivate hate and act as being the victim.

Thrive with your mind, be a genius, prevent problems. Procrastination is like becoming in debt with time and the interest rate is brutally high. Often, people procrastinate because they don't have a plan. Always plan the difficult while it's easy. Everything you delay will become more difficult. Lose the excuses and find your results because there's always a reason not to do something. Don't wait to harvest the pineapple while it's sweet. Everything left for later, when you have the chance to do it now, often leads to regrets.

Later, the coffee gets cold.
Later, you lose interest.
Later, the day turns into night.
Later, people grow up.
Later, people grow old.
Later, life goes by.

Love the pineapple you have now before life teaches you about the ananas you've lost.

Truthful is fruitful

Charlie Chaplin
If you're truly truthful to yourself, it's wonderful guidance.

A philosophic statement of The Pineapple Theory to influence harmony with the purpose of achieving freedom, *feel & think* with balance, and thrive at achieving pineHappliness is as follows: Be kind and truthful and life will be fruitful. When used with aware consciousness and care, Truth is a compass that never fails.

- What if being truthful with yourself means you see yourself outside of your emotional illusions with *life & time?*
- What if being truthful with yourself means you are peaceful with yourself?
- What if being truthful with yourself means you are the person you should be, meaning you are not making your life more difficult for no good reason by being someone you are not?

What if being truthful with yourself means you can think, and engage in a clear reasoning process, inspiring your self-confidence with the fact that the positive solution is you? Again, your thoughts are your own cure and *placebo.* The above series of self-reflective questions are intended to think for yourself to always better find yourself, which is a must when the daily negative pressure acts like a blur in the emotional illusions. Using the concept of *Coaching with the Extreme Obvious*, let me share the following perspectives speaking Chaplin's quotation along with the series of self-reflective questions.

A person with an alcohol, drug, or gambling addiction admits truthfully to themselves they have an addiction problem. That's how they start becoming their own cure. Unless accepted by themselves from their own conclusion, one will resist what they are told.

Let me apply the self-realization concept by sharing more about my COVID-19 furlough experience. I previously shared I quickly updated my resume and started to apply for several open job positions when announced my furlough. With less than 1% response following about 50 submissions, when truthful with myself, I have sought within for positive solutions that would profit from a positive outcome around. Therefore, it was not about living thinking my resume was perfect and employers were the problem, rather, it was a signal to keep improving my resume to make it stand out like a pineapple. I paid a consultant to update my resume, then later observed an increase in responses from employers. This short example connects how we *feel & think* because when you seek within, you truly guide yourself.

Speak your truth with clarity. It starts with *why*, there's vulnerability, and there's lessons learned. I'm always at the top of my *positive curiosity* with people speaking as if everything is perfect because they often have the worst demons within. The most impactful non-verbal exhibited is one scratching their face when responding that everything is perfect.

Does truth truly harm others?

What if many can't handle the truth because the truth is either not properly shared, or because they are conditioned of hearing *comforting lies, emotional lies,* or *rational lies* with themselves. The truth often "harms" people persisting in self-deceit and ignorance. All truth passes through three stages:

- First, it is ridiculed.
- Second, it's attacked or opposed.
- Third, it's accepted as being self-evident.

9 September 2023, I posted the following on social media, speaking the third stage: *"Of course something you did not know is obvious once heard, or read about."* Meaning that, the truth is taken for granted, and if you ever do me the honor to read my book *The Art of Life Museum*, the exhibition hall The Art of Truth will widen your perspective. Also, the 3 stages is an experience when someone shares an idea, and the fundamental anchor preventing the 3 emotional stages is, *be positively curious.*

Sometimes people don't want to hear the truth because they don't want their illusions destroyed, and all fixed set patterns are incapable of adaptability or pliability. The truth is outside of all fixed patterns like what freedom is passed your fears. I'm no comedian, but here's a funny example many will likely relate with:

Your life partner: *"Did I gain weight?"*
Your response: *"What do your clothes say?"*

Remember the following: When you live with your inner child, you're an honest person, meaning that you are true to yourself, and can't be false to anyone. The same must live within, be true to yourself because calling the truth a lie is criminal.

Although this book's manuscript assembles several pieces, previously shared, my books are like a Lego set, and I share several perspectives inspired by them. Reading over again my published work, perspectives about living truthfully are found everywhere, and it's not a coincidence. Like a pineapple today loved and with a fruitful history and legacy, what if your honesty could be the recipe for a rich legacy?

I often speak about our inner child because it greatly serves at understanding humans better along with how to live more "pineHapply", together. Since I launched my first book of The Pineapple Theory, I learned to live with my inner child, giving me a blossom inner Freedom and Peace with more Love because – in part - an honest person is always a child. Meaning, the day I became stronger than my selfish ego, everything else surrounding me became more Peaceful & Loving, giving a true thriving Freedom with myself. Yes, the Freedom of yourself that is. In life, if we are true to ourselves, we cannot be false to anyone, and an unbreakable integrity gives real freedom because there's nothing to fear since there's nothing to hide.

Often shared, your thoughts are you because you are your thoughts meaning you are your own *placebo* because mistakes – for example – are always forgivable when truthfully accepted & acknowledged by one-self, meaning that unless one comes to their own self-realization and conclusion truthfully and with reasoning, one will deny nearly everything and will have excuses for everything. Including with mistakes by others, the truthful one will demonstrate strength by seeking their own mistakes within the mistakes of others. Word of cautious though, a mistake happening more than once is no longer a mistake, it's a habit requiring fixing.

But, admitting our mistake – if not trained – is no child play. Here's why:

The hardest words to say are, "I was wrong." People would rather lie and pull themselves further in the abyss than face that sentence because admitting failure threatens their identity, and we protect our identity with everything we've got. This is raw *cognitive dissonance* when reality conflicts with a person's self-image, especially if they've invested time, status or emotion *(Ikea Effect).* The brain doesn't correct the course; it rewrites the story. Admitting they were wrong isn't just uncomfortable, it threatens identity status, even belonging. So instead, the brain twists logic to defend the choice, and the worse the outcome, the more justification it needs. They're not blind deep down. They see the truth but admitting it would make them feel like the biggest fool. Speaking volume about why a lie hates to be challenged.

A working solution to make someone let go of bad beliefs is: Don't Give them a version of the story that saves their ego, offer a narrative that lets them change without feeling like a traitor to themselves. A "hard solution" is like confronting fear; corner them with truth that makes their current self-image unbearable. *Sooooory,* but people don't change when you prove them wrong, they change when the cost of staying wrong becomes higher than their pride can carry.

That said, if you seek freedom, I strongly suggest becoming honest and truthful with yourself for the following reason: Relief yourself from the negative emotional weight of what you try to cover up, from trying to save face, and from protecting a false pride just to showcase a good image of yourself. The more you wait and keep covering up or protecting a lie with yourself, the heavier the covers become. Humans often make life more complicated than it is because they try to live a life that is not theirs. Seinfeld's George Constanza is a brilliant example of this. Eventually, it becomes toxic for one's life because they know that truth will eventually destroy them, and they end up trying to destroy others with their lies.

The previous suggested thought is important because sadly, there may be laws stopping one from being free with themselves, meaning they are in the wrong environment, and their true solution is to change their environment. If you are *positively curious* with people who relocated, and are an active listener to their story, you will understand the pattern shared in this paragraph.

From my careful observation at detecting emotional patterns with tens of thousands of years with our emotional timeline, I'm challenged at observing the following differently:

Society can't accept the truth because they are not taught how to speak the truth efficiently, and because most of society live the lives of others without even truly understanding what they *meme*, they are falsely guided and influenced.

I'll be thought provocative for a moment: A top tier ego & selfish wealthy living lies with themselves to build themselves will buy the media for them to also speak their lies becoming a poor education for society. The backfire of this is from the portion of society who – most of the time – can live truthfully, they lose trust towards influential people, and with the most influential voice, the media. Then what? When a truth is exposed in justice about a top influential person living with lies becoming society's blindness, it's better to risk sparing a guilty person rather than to condemn an innocent one. It's challenging for a liar to seek balance because when they speak the truth, they are not listened.

I know I'm repeating myself, it's lengthy, and it's likely the consequence of soul aging but also because I can't repeat enough in life. Here's another perspective about why I'm challenged to observe differently:

There are patterns with our *emotional timeline* exhibiting that many people can't handle the truth. From a high-level view, people can't handle it because they are not properly educated at accepting it, and many people poorly communicate becoming a challenge and conflict to experience more peace & love. With my theory, I suggest experiencing life as much as possible like a *guinea pig,* and to always practice the fundamental anchors to see & understand ourselves & life outside of the emotional illusions with *life & time*. Not only can you master yourself more, but you also can find the truth within because truth be told, no one will truly pour the truth in you. Again, and always, life is a do-it-yourself project, you must surround yourself with the right people and always have one <u>living</u> resource of wisdom who can share with you a truth the way you wish to be told the truth. All truth from a wise mind will become your road map, within, to find the most fruitful and sweetest pineapple plantation in you. It's like a modern Treasure.

It amazes me how people don't realize how hard it is to speak the truth to a world full of people that don't realize they're living a lie with themselves, and a lie influenced by their surroundings. Since thousands of years with our timeline that we live in times of universal deceit, and speaking the truth is felt like a revolutionary act. Living truthfully is living freely within and around. It can be viewed as a main path to dealing with an unfree world, then the freedom of your existence will be viewed as an act of rebellion. It reminds about several American sitcoms which include a "weird" or peculiar main character, and the more the audience learn about the "weird", the more it's their preferred character. The interpreted message is as follows: The "weird" lives to their true self, not a lie.

With my ongoing careful observation with our emotional timeline with *life & time*, I come to the conscious realization that I simply can't keep letting society repeat a modernized past without doing something about it, inspiring the philosophies and perspectives harvested with my work of The Pineapple Theory to cultivate more thriving and pineHapply people.

The first step of a courageous person is not to take part in a lie. An example of this would be as follows: Defending someone who's liked instead of defending what is right. You see, shutting your eyes and mind to what are facts truly is lazy and cowardly, meaning that we must always train ourselves to become stronger to endure a difficult life. In fact, we live life with the desire of happiness, and life challenges us with pain. It's life's job, it's not cruel, but a path to growth. If you are an endeavor believer, pray for the strength to endure a difficult life, but make it a calling for yourself, then do something about it because it's a do-it-yourself project, there aren't any magic beans because no one truly is coming to save you.

In life, you will always harvest what you planted, and you'll be challenged at living your life with an inner peace and freedom if you are not truthful. I suggest free yourself in life, be truthful with yourself. Word of cautious though, you own your positive solution, and I insist with the following self-reflective filter shared in a few books of mine before you choose to act with your solution:

- Is it free of all forms of Hate?
- Is it free of Division?
- Is it free of all forms of Harm?
- Is it compliant with the books of rules?
- Is it inspired from what facts are, meaning free of what could emotionally trick you such as: What you think is, should, could, assume, and not source from gossip?

Truth be told again, life gives us hard truth reaching the *trust threshold*, and when seeking more Freedom – Peace - and Love with yourself may require cleaning house. Meaning, change your surroundings and your own thinking. My mentorship tip is to move on like you never knew them because you didn't truly know them. Here are some random perspectives about this:

With yourself
If you give one respect based on fear, you have disrespected yourself, and in life, one of your worst sins is often when you destroy and betray yourself for nothing.

From others, and yourself
It is easier to forgive an enemy than to forgive a friend, but how about yourself? Can you forgive yourself? When a friend hurts you, it truly sucks, and that is likely because you can't trust them anymore, that's a frustration. A friend that hurts you is often the person you expected the least to hurt you, so when it happens, it easily disturbs your inner peace.

With my books, I speak the analogy & metaphor of *the emotional fisherman*, defined as one fishing your emotions, and it's nothing positive. *The emotional fisherman* is often weak, insecure, immature, and becoming narcissistic and toxic for one's life. Some *emotional fishermen* – often experienced in the workplace and powerful with the competition universe of Politics – will escalate things as follows; because they cannot manipulate you, they try to control how others view you. Many will also make insults their tool when they know a debate is lost.

Someone truthful with themselves doesn't need to play mind games with others, and no negotiation is required to enter one's heart. When facing this smooth positivity truthfully, you pineHapply thrive, and that's sweet & fruitful like a pineapple.

Based on life's *Law of Balance,* you'll always find something much better than what was not meant to be. That's true only if you let go of your emotional slavery with open eyes to give eye to your mind. Think about this; how miserable is one begging for love? Without love, there's a gap that can only be filled with respect – kindness – and good manners & etiquette serving as a substitution for love. When one or more is broken, trust is broken. When trust is broken, please create a mental picture of a beautiful authentic glass to serve the sweetest and tastiest fresh pineapple juice, and then picture the glass broken in pieces. Even if you glue it back together, it will never be the same, you forced it. That's what a beggar does…

- They could not have self-control.
- They were slave to their emotions and pleasures.
- They were ready to lose everything for something they did not have.
- They come back after they disappointed others.
- They thought they were better than you, and they are asking for everything to be forgiven.

Remember this about people in life; as soon as you accept this type of behavior, you are accepting them to behave this way with you, and that often leads to a loss of yourself. It's like allowing once to a cat to jump on the kitchen table, you allowed it once, and there's sadly no going back. Or it's like a black hole in space; it starts small, and the more it sucks, the more it expands.

From my observations, I must share that the following speaks important patterns about people not living truthfully with themselves, becoming conflicts with themselves and others. For example, and not limited to:

- From my 25+ years supporting companies with investigative services, the following always happened: Many people claim to be a victim of one's reaction and will only tell what one did, and not what they said or did to pissed one off.
- When I coach and mentor, there's always a small portion (1%-3%) sticking to the following: Most ignorance is vincible – avoidable - ignorance, and many don't know because they don't want to know.
- We swallow greedily any lie that flatters us, but we sip only little by little at a truth we find bitter.
- I view that living truthfully is by never blaming others for what you don't do yourself.
- I observed that to anger an honest person, lie to them, but to anger a narcissist,

tell them the truth.

- And lastly, a common one: Between what is said and not meant, and what is meant and not said, most trust is lost.

As the leader of your life and captain of your boat, never forget that you will always be responsible for how you act, no matter how you feel. Meaning, never make someone pay the emotional price because you could not manage positively, your own emotions. Understanding this means that you *seek within* and are truthful with yourself. I often share that in life, how you choose to *Think-Act-Speak* is all you and no one else, it's 100% your responsibility, including with how you resonate with the inner voice of an all mighty from the belief of your choosing because it's about how you are using it.

Never lie to yourself and you'll thrive. Your growth in life will be proportional to the amount of truth you can accept about yourself without running away.

Your mind is your temple. Your truth is your compass. And when you stop overthinking and start living with clarity, you rise. Fruitfully.

Be kind. Be truthful. And life will be fruitful. That's not just a philosophy, it's your crown, and many don't dare wearing this type of crown.

Make the Call

London 2022 – Copyright Steve "Mr. Pineapple Mathieu – Original picture by Hozir Sahdat

Chinese proverb
A wise man makes his own decision; an ignorant man follows public opinion.

Earlier, I revealed to you several failures for growth with my books, and when I released my title *Worldwide fruitful travels with a pineapple,* it bridged and glued The Pineapple Theory and most importantly, the pineapple fruit blended with my books.

I'm often asked, *"why the pineapple",* and with several titles, I'm also often asked *"which book should I read first"?* With currently 10 books of mine available – for now – many experiences a *decision paralysis* which a valuable aspect about humans' psychology to understand in business.

Decision paralysis is the inability to decide out of fear of making the wrong choice or being overwhelmed by too many options.

Though, it may explain - in perspective - the importance of the *shiny effect* meaning that with many options, beauty like an impactful book title and cover will win before taste. True in a bookstore in a world with likely more book titles than there are readers. With this perspective in mind, if you don't hold people's hand and guide them where to go, they freeze, and many are somehow becoming *Buridan's donkey.*

If you are not familiar with *Buridan's donkey:* It suggests that a hungry donkey placed between two bales will die because it can't decide. As for *the shiny effect,* it suggests our preference for shiny things is linked to our need for water. They believe that every person's preference for shininess has deep evolutionary roots and that we are attracted to things that serve a purpose for fulfilling our innate needs.

When I mentor people who are expressing, or exhibiting, a *decision paralysis*, I speak of *Buridan's donkey.* Then, I suggest the following seed for thoughts to cultivate their decision making: Add a third option. Coincidentally, a third option gives life to my *Theoretical Three* fundamental anchor. Making a clear decision – making the call – is important with yourself because maybe is – and *sooooory* – coward. People don't follow uncertainty, they follow finality. You can't shape your reality by suggesting, you shape it by declaring because when you say something with conviction, your brain registers it as truth and more importantly, so does everyone else. Psychology calls this *The Illusion of Finality,* a bias that makes people accept firm confident statements as reality even without evidence. Influential people don't speak "I think" or "I'm not sure", they say how it is. Great negotiation doesn't stand tall on "maybe we could do this", but with "here's what's going to happen." The tone alone changes. Weak language invites debate. Strong language close it.

If you want influence, make the call. Stop using conditional speech. Stop diluting your intent with maybe, I guess, I think per The Pineapple Theory's anchors. Say it with confidence like it's already a law, like the person whose words sound like decisions, not suggestions.

Like a captain, you must make the call; go right, left, or straight ahead. Like in the 2008 movie, The Dark Knight, you must make the call: it's one or the other. Every day, as soon as you open your eyes, you must make the following call: Are you going to have a great or a bad day?

Your life will be defined by your ability to handle uncertainty. Sometimes, your gut feeling will guide you but often, you can establish the most favorable call to make requiring your *positive curiosity.* Most tools from the time management serving of this book can assist. And here's a friendly awareness about your gut feeling because it speaks from the Soil of The Pineapple Theory.

"Trust your gut" feels empowering, but psychological research shows it is one of the most dangerous decision-making strategies. Gut feelings are not pure intuition; they are heavily contaminated by cognitive biases. That's a big *soooory* moment!

Take the *Availability Heuristic* (Tversky & Kahneman, 1973): we judge the likelihood of events by how easily examples come to mind. See constant posts about people striking it rich with a meme coin, and your "gut" tells you it's a good investment, even if the base rate of success is near zero.

Or the *Halo Effect* (Thorndike, 1920): one positive trait, such as attractiveness or confidence, unconsciously colors our entire judgment of a person. This is why people hire charismatic but incompetent employees or fall for partners they later regret.

Then there's *Confirmation Bias* (Nickerson, 1998): our tendency to search for, interpret, and remember information that supports what we already want to believe. If you want a stock to be a winner, your gut highlights every supportive sign while ignoring glaring red flags.

What people call intuition is often just biased pattern recognition. Nobel laureate Daniel Kahneman (2011) showed that unless you have deep expertise in a stable domain (like a firefighter reading smoke), intuition is rarely trustworthy. For most decisions, your "gut" is simply replaying distorted shortcuts. And a proposed antidote is systems and evidence:

Be positively curious; write pros and cons, consult external opinions, and commit to rules before emotions strike. Decisions grounded in verifiable data outperform gut-driven ones in almost every domain.

When I presented you with my prioritization tool, baseline topics were a generic sample and not a full list of targets. I have though, sometimes and often used in Risk Management, completed the PESTLE analysis taught in Business Management which upgraded the main rationalization for keeping focus with the end goal, with a ranking. My project for my title, *Worldwide fruitful travels with a pineapple* had Waikiki in Hawaii, and I canceled it because of risk factors which turned out to become reality like a general labor strike in hotels, hurricane, and more. This wasn't gut feeling, but data driven. If you don't know about PESTLE, here's an introduction.

PESTLE-Analysis is a framework used to scan an organization's external environment. Political, Economic, Social, Technological, Legal, and Environmental stands for PESTLE with the purpose of identifying key factors from the wider, uncontrollable external environment that might affect an organization. Like everything in life, there are pros & cons (*Law of Balance*) to using the PESTLE-Analysis to help plan an organizational strategy.

Pro
It provides a simple and easy-to-use framework for your analysis. It helps to reduce the impact and effects of potential threats to an organization and provides a mechanism that enables an organization to identify and exploit new opportunities.

Con
Users can oversimplify the information that is used for making decisions. Also, the process must be conducted regularly to be effective and often, organizations do not make this investment.

One more tool I highly recommend practicing is also taught in business management and called, the DECIDE model by academic researcher from University of Hawaii–West Oahu, Kristina Guo. Talk about Hawaii being a peculiar coincidence, right?

The DECIDE model was intended to as a resource for health care managers when applying the crucial components of decision-making, but it also enables managers to improve their decision-making skills, which leads to more effective decisions.
The DECIDE model is the acronym for 6 specific activities needed in the decision-making process:

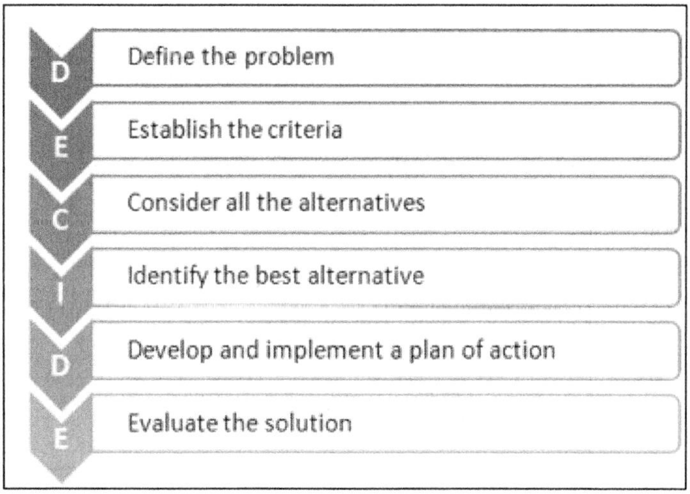

<u>Define the Problem</u>
Make sure to define what you want to achieve. Your positive curiosity with your surroundings will add thriving value as they may share different perspectives on the best solutions.

<u>Establish the criteria</u>
Collect some information (investigate): What information is needed, the best sources of information, and how to get it. Both internal and external work are to be considered. Seeking it through a process of self-assessment is internal. Research online, in books, from people, and from other sources is external.

Consider all the alternatives
The better options you consider, the more comprehensive your final decision will be. When you generate alternatives, you push yourself to look at the problem from different angles like changing path to reach a goal because the goal will not change. Feasibility, risks, and implications of each choice must be considered. By evaluating the risk involved with various options, you can determine whether the risk is manageable and if resources are adequate.

Identify the best alternative
Choose between the alternatives by comparing all the choices you have and determine the relative importance of various factors.
Develop and implement a plan of action
With the purpose of building self-confidence with your selection, truer when it must be explained to people involved in implementing your decision, talk about why you chose the alternative because the more information you provide about risk and projected benefits, the more likely people are to support the decision.

Evaluate the solution
Lastly, consider the results of your decision and evaluate whether it has resolved the need you identified in step 1, or not. Going back to the drawing board is an English proverb, and there's what you will need to do if you have not reached your goal. You may need to deep dive more and consult more perspectives to inspire you more.

Before moving on to the next chapter, remember the following: Big decisions deserve your clearest thinking; not your strongest feelings. With a thought provocative approach, making your own right decisions is wisdom, following society's opinions and what is popular is ignorance.

And when making decisions, careful when ego and drained emotional batteries are at the decision discussion, they are the reason for the following classic: "Let me sleep on it". Here's why:

All day, you stay disciplined; eat clean, focus, say no to distractions. But late in the day, you're binging snacks, doomscrolling, or texting people you swore you'd cut off. The reason isn't weakness. It's *Ego Depletion:* the idea that willpower functions like a muscle and gets fatigued with use.
Every act of self-control throughout the day drains your "mental battery." By night, that battery is close to empty. That's why studies show people resist temptations more successfully in the morning, but by evening, impulsivity takes over (Baumeister et al., 1998; Hagger et al., 2010). In fact, even minor acts of choice or restraint slowly wear down your capacity to regulate yourself, leaving you vulnerable when it matters most. Solutions?

- Front-load decisions: Sign contracts, resolve conflicts, or make commitments earlier in the day.
- Automate the small stuff: Reduce trivial choices (meals, routines) so you conserve willpower because once a behavior is encoded in procedural memory

through repetition (see: Duhigg, The Power of Habit, 2012), it runs on autopilot, bypassing the need for daily motivation. James Clear (2018).

- Sleep as a reset: Rest restores self-regulation. "Sleep on it" is more than a proverb, it's neuroscience.

Respect your crown. Respect your brain's limits. And you stop being sabotaged by late-night impulses like making wrongs calls. Every decision is a declaration. Every declaration is a direction. And when you make the call with clarity, you rise. Fruitfully.

8

Pineapple cultivation Thriving habits

You must let go of old habits that could hold you back at thriving with your progress.

The pineapple fruit, the jewel of the jungle. Of all fruits, it's life's finest art exhibition. When placed in a mixed plate of fruits, standing tall, all other fruits look much more fruitful. It has a sweet and peculiar history to learn from. It's a *Fibonacci* number for the math enthusiast. It's a swinger's invitation for types of enthusiasts. For me, it's my muse to cultivate pineHapply, and absolutely anything & everything about this majestic fruit is used to create analogies & metaphors.

For example, from its seed until ready to be harvested, the ananas growth process follows fixed patterns. The pineapple is a *multiple fruit,* meaning it is a compound fruit formed through the fusion of a cluster of flowers called an inflorescence, growing on a catkin, with each flower on the catkin producing a fruit, and the entire cluster maturing into a single mass meaning, the pineapple which ripens five to six months after flowering begins. Each fruitlet develops from a hermaphrodite flower, which is self-sterile, although it has both male and female parts. Self-sterility is advantageous in terms of fruit quality and palatability. The communication of fruitlet connection through the fruit core is crucial for fruit development and quality.

Pineapple's growth process is an inherited pattern, a growth habit, and humans are the same because everybody has recurring behavior patterns. Often though, humans are attached to their comfort zone with their occurring habits, and because they don't update themselves, they become limited to new results. Everything people do isn't driven by logic; it's driven by repetition. It's right, not because it's the best choice, but because the brain clings to patterns. They don't think, they follow the path they've already walked a thousand times before. They brain is designed for efficiency, not for change. Every repeated action strengthens neural pathways making behaviors automatic. This explains why bad habits feel impossible to break and why good habits take so much effort to form. The mind resists change because change is energy, and the brain is designed to conserve energy. Every decision. it makes is a calculation and which option requires the least effort. That when people behave per a psychological concept called, The Path of Least Resistance. People just follow the crowd and choose mediocrity. The harder something feels, the less likely they'll do it. If we reframe a change with the Law of Balance, we become part of someone's routine by attaching our presence, influence, and idea to what already feels natural to them (walking hand-by-hand). People don't change because they should; they change because the road leads them there. And if you lead yourself in life – being proactive instead of proactive – you build your own road and walk on it with your pineapple crown.

Here's an example from the above heavy chewing.

Earth was once on "time out" in 2020. For nearly all countries, everyone was asked to stay home. A simple ask, a simple positive mitigation measure for which everyone owned, and everyone could, together. A simple ask that was not intended for one to think for themselves – rather - it was simply asked because it was not about one. Inform humans they can't have something, and humans want it more than ever. In psychology and I'll repeat myself again, it's referred to as *reactance*, and it suggests that when people feel their freedom of choice or action is threatened or restricted, they experience a motivational state aimed at reclaiming that freedom, often leading to behaviors that are the opposite of what they are pressured to do.

When used correctly, you can make people want to think or do exactly what you do by simply framing what you want them to believe as something they may not understand, or something they may not be open to. *Reactance* then activates, and they will do everything to understand it, or to be open to it. Because my books of The Pineapple Theory stand alone in their niche, I must consistently apply this method when I meet with potential readers who then end up purchasing a copy, and they are pineHapply when doing so.

About COVID-19 and humans attached to their comfort zone with their occurring patterns; I lived in the Greater Montreal area, and a curfew was mandated at the first wave. Suddenly, it was at a peak time that many wanted to go out for a walk at night. Some even went to court asking to be exempt because they did not want to temporally change an emotional pattern.

Lack of abundance and humans will often think for themselves. In North America, toilet paper disruption… must I share more? In perspective, abundance is like a dog with food. Always have food available for a dog and it will consume what it needs. Feed the dog on schedule and it will clean its bowl like an Olympic 50-meter sprinter! *The dog with food concept* also applies in the workplace. Supply employees with abundance and they will think less about themselves. In psychology, it is referred to as *loss aversion*, and it suggest the fear of losing something, or the tendency to feel the pain of a loss more strongly than the pleasure of an equivalent gain. A psychological concept often shared already with this books.

What if I told you that over 90% of everything you do isn't your choice?

You think you're in control, but your subconscious made the decision before you even realized it. Every action, every desire, every so-called choice was already determined, your conscious mind is just here to justify it. You reach for your phone without thinking and you judge a person in milliseconds like when shopping for your fruit, and you will experience the *Halo effect,* or the *Horn effect.* Your conscious mind is just there to rationalize decisions your subconscious already made. Scientists found that brain activity predicting a decision happens seconds before you consciously choose. It's running on pre-programmed habits, emotions, and impulses reactions shaped by experience social conditioning and genetic instincts. When limited by old habits, if you want to change your life, don't fight your subconscious but reprogram it like a holistic re-wiring process. The right inputs, the right environments, the right habits, the right influences.

Classical conditioning was the first fundamental anchor I have shared with you, and here's why it's a valuable currency in psychology to influence new behaviors.

Classical conditioning, also called Pavlov's conditioning, must be understood and the study behind it is as follows, and please, word of cautious; use each persuasion technique from a place of good because it's powerful.

Accidentally discovered like several scientific breakthroughs, Ivan Petrovich Pavlov (1849–1936) was a physiologist, not a psychologist.

During the 1890s, Pavlov researched salivation in dogs in response to being fed. To measure saliva when the dogs were fed, he inserted a small test tube into the cheek of each dog. Pavlov predicted the dogs would salivate in response to the food in front of them, but he noticed that his dogs would begin to salivate whenever they heard the footsteps of their assistant, who was bringing them the food. He later discovered that any object or event which the dogs learned to associate with food would trigger the same response.

The psychology research by Pavlov started from the idea that there are some things that a dog does not need to learn. For example, dogs don't learn to salivate whenever they see food. This reflex is hard-wired into the dog meaning that food is an unconditioned stimulus, and salivation is an unconditioned response.

Pavlov used a metronome (a bell) as his neutral stimulus. By itself, the metronome did not elicit a response from the dogs. The conditioning procedure then began whereby the clicking metronome was introduced just before he gave food to his dogs. After several repeats of this procedure, he presented the metronome on its own.

The outcome is that the dogs had learned an association between the metronome and the food, and a new behavior had been learned. Because this response was learned - or conditioned - it is called a *conditioned response* also known as a *Pavlovian response*. The neutral stimulus has become a conditioned stimulus. Pavlov's finding is fundamental to understand our habits better and how we can re-wire ourselves. Here are examples about how I have applied Pavlov's conditioning to promote engagement in the workplace.

As I'm writing this book, I'm still an active Loss Prevention (LP) professional for companies, for more than 20 years. Like with the publication of my books, I've made tons of mistakes. I broke free by accepting them and learned to improve my style and philosophy. A process making me today an expert and someone people are seeking expertise and perspective from.

I'm often asked what an LP partner does, and my big picture response is; I assist companies at protecting their products, DATA, and most important of all, their people. I accomplish this purpose by coaching business leaders with best practices, with their policies and procedures, and I seek continuous improvement opportunities with their processes and procedures to improve how they can protect their products, DATA, and people. Their growth continuum becomes their greatness becoming a business culture.

In psychology, *positive reinforcement* suggests that adding a desirable stimulus or reward after a behavior increases the likelihood of that behavior being repeated. It's a core concept in operant conditioning, a type of learning where behaviors are shaped by their consequences.

Positive reinforcement was a power tool of mine with my last two employers, also referred as client, because this approach supported an efficient and successful *CHECK* process of the company LP Program. To complement your knowledge, the principle for any program follows the following structure: Plan – Define – Check – Act.

When I worked in airports with the purpose to promote an engaging LP & Safety Culture, I remember before boarding an aircraft to visit my assigned US locations, I made sure to purchase a few boxes of Canadian Maple Cream cookies. They are delicious! As I visited stores and engaged with the associates, I created games to challenge them with their LP & Safety knowledge. Not only were we having fun doing it, what they did not know about LP & Safety was coached efficiently, and the reward of earning their delicious Canadian Maple Cream cookies made the learning of LP & Safety a more positive & efficient process. It was welcoming with the hospitality of a pineapple. Other times, I had gift cards in my jacket, challenging their knowledge with a different game and the more they knew, the more chances they had to win the raffle at the end of my visit and be rewarded, have their picture taken, and posted in the location's monthly newsletter with the story about why & how the associate was being recognized. This helped to influence everyone's learning. As a result, not only was there a higher engagement level, but the *CHECK* process was also completed, and growth opportunities were shared with the leadership team without feeling any resentment from them. In my first year of service, I was awarded with Best Shrink result, and the field team had been conditioned to view me as positive in their heart & mind.

In the field of LP & Safety, there is behind the scenes work, such as data analytics. I call it; the *"Safety Net."* A discrete layer of the *Loss Prevention-in-depth* strategy. Culture was in my perspective the pro-active approach, and the *Safety Net* served to efficiently help identify dishonest, at risk, and suspicious behaviors. When detected, identified, and confirmed, the ACT stage comes in play, meaning feedback must be provided to the worker by management or an LP & Safety field manager. How we approach the feedback process will be valuable to ensure *positive reinforcement.* The *platinum rule of empathy* must be remembered along with the fundamental anchor that every behavior originates from a Desire – Motive – Opportunity. Mistakes happen and forgetting a Best Practice happens as well. By approaching the workers successes first and then approaching the feedback process helping the worker becoming more efficient and successful, works great.

An example of a game played with field associates.

Another example is from 2021 when I launched Amazon's East Canada delivery stations (Last Mile division). Several managers had never collaborated with a Loss Prevention partner before and for me, building a foundation truly was my priority to influence long term results. It's like investing money properly; then money works for you. There also I often engaged the field team with games and rewards. Then, I experimented the following: On my mobile worktable, I had the following desk bell and a note guiding to ring if they needed a touch of happiness. When people tapped on it, I happily voiced, "happiness" while dancing a little. The day I stopped carrying my desk bell, just crossing eyes with people made them feel happier.

Smile desk bell for anchoring and conditioned a behavior/ emotion

In a motivational speech to the not-for-profit Engineers of Tomorrow, I shared that I'm emotionally engaged with superheroes and humor. I often watch re-runs of classic sitcoms, and I quickly identify common scenes or episodes speaking topics I have in mind – or once written - and because they are watched by millions, it influences a more efficient persuasion by establishing *similarity*. You can discover, made with humor, variants of Pavlov's experiment with the following sitcoms:

The Office (American version): Season 3, episode 15.
The Big Bang Theory: Season 3, episode 3.
Seinfeld: Season 9, episode 4.

Classical conditioning is a fundamental anchor because it surrounds us all the time and that is true if one accepts to see it from our timeline. Before sharing additional real-life *guinea pig* experience of mine, allow me to deep dive into a philosophic perspective about *classical conditioning*. If Pavlov started from the idea that there are some things that a dog does not need to learn because several unconditioned stimuli influence their behaviors and reactions as an unconditioned response, what if the *similarity principle* applies for humans? I researched in my text journal and found the following inspiration. Please meet Puppy Arnold!

It was 2013 when puppy Arnold was entertaining my life. I remember the very first time I played fetch with Arnold. Without teaching him how, he simply ran to the toy, ran back like a boomerang, and from time-to-time, giving it back or I had to chase for it. Along with playing fetch, puppy Arnold started to naturally do a signature move for a pug: Looking to your eyes while their head band to the side as if they are questioning you!

For puppy Arnold to fetch and band his head on the side was not taught or influenced. It was natural (unconditioned) behavior. Theoretically in the emotional illusions with *life & time*, what if at their birth, humans already have the instinct about what is emotionally negative, and emotionally positive? Like a pineapple seed unconditioned to become a pineapple plant. What should become is positively cultivated for a growth continuum.

I shared earlier that in the emotional illusions with *life & time,* your true self is right there, buried under cultural conditioning, other people's opinions, and inaccurate conclusions you drew as a child and adult that became/influences your beliefs about who you are. All can trick you emotionally and if you don't take time to pause in your mind, define as your temple, resulting in losing yourself and forgetting yourself. Self-reflecting about The Pineapple Theory's purpose, there's a hidden *classical conditioning.* What if acting from a place of good making others smile, or feel great, or making them more positive is like a reward – conditioning – for acting from a place a good? What if because of life's conditioning, this is needed to bring back alive what is at birth, an unconditioned stimulus. With my philosophical mind, allow me to disturb your thoughts. Wouldn't this strongly speak Earth history, and timeline, with the emotional deep knowledge about humans with their Myths and Mythologies with the purpose of living positively and happily, together?

If you truly open your eyes and mind to my pineapple theory, I can ensure you can free yourself from a bad habit and reward yourself with the freedom of a new habit, all by yourself, and it truly is about self-conditioning, strength, and consistency defining your determination. Allow me to share the following short story.

<u>Sushi story</u>
Normally, I do not share names, and I hide any form of what is considered "division" by many, using words like: They, their, them, etc. For this small story about persuasion, I will share names because he's a close friend and if he's reading this book, I do not want him to feel like a *guinea pig* – rather – the story is an example about how persuasion is part of our daily life experience. Think of the times you have persuaded your life partner or a friend to do something when at first, you thought, or they did not feel like it.

Several years ago, I started enjoying eating sushi. From time to time, I ate them in front of my good friend Louis. He kept telling me that they did not look appetizing: *"Burk, raw fish and cold rice!"* he claimed, and I kept repeating to him that one day, he would enjoy eating sushi. Each time I was quoting this, I was "*scheming*" him with an upcoming emotion to expect.

In psychology, *scheming* often suggests a personality trait or behavior pattern characterized by manipulativeness, deceit, and a calculated, cynical view of others, potentially linked to Machiavellianism or traits within the "dark triad".

Eventually, I ate sushi again when he was with me, and I asked him (my friends and I are giving each other names): *"Loulou, you enjoy what is fried. Try this piece, only this one, it is warm, crispy, and its chicken inside."* Because I established *similarities*, he did eat the one piece of sushi offered and he liked it, even more when dipped in spicy mayo. At that time, there was no going back, he had taken one definite step forward leading to thousands of steps forward. Like eating a full pineapple, eat it one sweet, bite at a time. After he had eaten that one piece of sushi, I shared with him: *"See, you like sushi, you just don't know yet about it. Start with rolls containing what you like, that is how I started."* This statement made me the tester, and he was the King.

Since he had eaten one single piece of sushi, Louis eats every sushi available on the menu. This small story about persuasion and implementing a new habit applies to kids but often, we will try to hide a change from them. A love example of mine referred to psychology as the just *noticeable difference*, also known as *change blindness*, is from the loved sitcom The Big Bang Theory. Penny & Leonard are starting their journey of living together. Leonard learns from Sheldon that without noticing, Penny is hiding his collectable from their bedroom in a storage room item-by-item. Small changes that do not meet a *change noticeable threshold.*

In psychology, a *just noticeable difference*, also known as the *difference threshold,* refers to the smallest detectable difference between two stimuli that a person can notice about 50% of the time. This concept is central to psychophysics, the study of the relationship between physical stimuli and their perceived sensations.

You can thrive at self-installing a new habit with *semantic network* as your leverage and the sushi story is an example because when your actions don't align with your beliefs, you don't act differently, you change your beliefs. That's why smokers keep smoking, gamblers keep gambling, and why people defend terrible decisions. In psychology, it's referred to as *cognitive dissonance*, suggesting a psychological phenomenon where you feel discomfort when your behavior doesn't align with your values or beliefs, and for which your mind can't handle the tension. In life, everything starts with you, like altering your beliefs to make your actions seem justified if you want someone to stay committed to a choice. The secret is like eating a pineapple one sweet bite at the time, meaning to take a small action in that direction. To start, first time action will have your mind justify it, and the more you repeat that action and thought, then the identity changes leading to a big commitment. Free trials, political indoctrination, even Cults explains why they work so well. The mind hates inconsistency, it's always seeking a comfort zone, so it rewrites reality to stay congruent.

In life, and let's speak the truth, we all have bad habits and many of them are motivated from elementary behaviors shared in my suggested conclusion. You see, bad habits truly are easy to form and hard to live with, like losing our freedom from our negative thinking, and good habits are hard to form, but easy to live with. Control your mind – or – Be controlled by your mind was shared earlier with your reading, and it applies to habits as follows: Control your habits – or – Be controlled by your habits.

A personal example of mine, which many can relate to, was the bad habit of drinking one (1) glass of red wine at the end of a hard day of labor before dinner, sitting on the sofa, watching the news and updating social media for The Pineapple Theory. I have done it for about 4 years, daily. One day, without planning for it, I skipped this habit, and I felt my brain and body reacting as if something was missing. When I watched the time, it was when I normally sat for a glass of red wine. That's when I knew it was a bad habit. I had become *Pavlov's dog* generating more saliva when the bell was heard, but no food was served. Meaning, I had conditioned myself to a habit.

Simply shared about the psychology of habits, it's like the exterior texture of a pineapple, yes, a pineapple analogy alert because after all, it is The Pineapple Theory. Carefully observe a pineapple shell, its exterior, and you will realize that it looks like a network, meaning connected dots because of *multiple fruit.* A habit is often from 2 concepts that appear together in space & time becoming connected, and the 2 concepts make a dot. An example of my bad habit would be (1) drinking a glass of red wine, and (2) sitting at a consistent time daily with a setting.

Because life is the positive & negative complementing each together, it means that to free yourself from a bad habit, you must substitute with, and cultivate a new habit becoming freedom, meaning the positive, and you are the positive solution, the balance, it's a do-it-yourself project. This process will work much more efficiently, and long-lasting if done like eating a full pineapple, meaning one sweet bite at a time. You could go "cold turkey", but chances of failure increases. Here's the principle to assist this process to self-condition yourself, like a reset or a re-wire of your engineering network, meaning your brain: Remove the cues from its 6 triggers, then replace the behavior.

Six triggers of a cue:

1. Emotion: I had a hard day of labor. I'll have a red glass of wine. With time, everyday becomes a hard day of labor!
2. Time: It's 5PM! It's time for a red glass of wine.
3. Location: In the comfort of a home or hotel bar.
4. People: Not applicable for me but do picture yourself enjoying your bad habit with colleagues or friends, like at a "Happy Hour".
5. Action: Watching the news and updating social media on my laptop.
6. Object: Having a bottle of wine at home, or a plain view at the hotel.

For me, what I have done, because I was able to make this change, is I moved my gym workout session from early morning to after work, becoming a time to release the intensity of work at the gym with weightlifting. The behavior was also fixed because after a proud weightlifting session, the thought for a glass of wine was kept away to keep the motion of healthiness, allowing me to update social media with my laptop sitting comfortably while watching the news before dinner. I substituted the action (or motion) of drinking with a big glass of chocolate milk or protein shake.

To replace a behavior, read again the Sushi Story, and apply a *noticeable difference,* an incremental change to progressively re-wire your brain and emotion to adapt to a new habit. The same applies in business for a large group of people. Before moving forward with the next topic, never forget that you are your worst enemy in life, and the process of resetting a habit comes with life's *law of balance.* With my book, *Feel & Think like a pineapple*, I share that our brain has two main sections, (1) emotional thinking and (2) rational thinking.

With the *law of balance*, your attempt to install a new habit will trigger your brain to trick you with *rational-lies* when you make use of your rational thinking, and *emotional-lies* when you make use of your emotional thinking. Both *rational-lies* and *emotional-lies* become *comforting-lies!* Often, shared with my books, and you read it with this book, the more you learn about yourself and about life, the more you can live freely with yourself because you can overcome yourself.

When working to install new habits, consistency is your determination and expect to engage in a battle of reasoning with yourself for which you must win with your objectives and goals. Keep focus. Always be stronger than yourself because you will experience the following with yourself, also my friends, the following is used as a power tool by Marketers because truth be told, Marketers are not trying to sell you something – rather – they are justifying why you should purchase.

Picture yourself at a happy hour with colleagues, or friends, and here's what you'll face if you've been free of a daily glass of wine for 2 weeks. Does the following *emotional-lies* and *rational lies* sound like familiar *comfort-lies*?

"It's only one drink."
"I need to drink, or I'll be boring."
"I've been good, I haven't had a drink in 2-weeks, I deserve it!"
"My colleagues are all here. I need a drink."
"It will look weird if I don't drink."

9

Pineapple love with an inner roar

When you love and are passionate about what you do, and the "why" you do it, you become unstoppable.

Philosophically, from my careful observation of more than tens of thousands of years with our timeline, I detected remarkable emotional patterns, and one of those patterns is that most humans lack curiosity with their emotions. Meaning that many don't invest energy in themselves, they don't care or don't have the courage to look at life beneath the surface, and many are ready to do the craziest things to avoid looking within themselves. The result, along with pointing fingers around and some people living with darkness in their heart, is all about whatever shines on the tip of the iceberg. In psychology, it's referred to as the *shiny effect.*

What people first see acts like their first fence. It's a cue for their emotional process and following a rapid spreading activation response building their emotions, their second fence will either activate for reasoning with curiosity or emotionally reject without knowledge. It's a hard truth about life and humans because for centuries, it's beauty before taste, like when people purchase their fruits. I refer to this fruitful behavior as the *psychology of fruits*, a variant of the following living pattern and philosophy: Many people invent, criticize, and accuse others when they never met them.

Every person we know exists only as a projection in our mind because we never see someone in every moment, every situation, or know the full depth of their thoughts. At best we grasp about 30% of whom a person truly is yet. our brain struggles with incomplete information (*curiosity gap*). So, it fills in the gaps on its own, creating an image that feels whole but is inevitably shaped by our own biases and assumptions. So, 70% is our own projection, our own idea of what this person is like, and it is precisely the 70% that ultimately disappoints because disappointment arises when expectations differ from reality. Nobody will act exactly like our projection of them, and that's why we are easily disappointed. It's not the person who disappoints us, but our own projection of them. People will always act in ways that align with who they are, not with the version we've imagined.

A fruit's appearance based on sets of standards is deep rooted from everything surrounding us since we were a child, it influences us to judge what makes a fruit look fresh, tasty, and cultivating the mental picture of enjoying it. The fruit's beauty example has deep roots within humans' psychology explaining the tough challenge major grocery chains had with the attempt to educate their customers that the quality of their "ugly" produce product line was not inferior. For society, it's sadly not taste before beauty; it's beauty before taste. Diving deeper into the *shiny effect* and *psychology of fruits*, is with what is referred to in psychology as, the *halo effect.* Because life is experienced with the *Law of Balance*, the *halo effect* evil twin is the *horn effect.*

The *halo effect* suggests that a positive impression in one area of a person, brand, or product can influence one's overall perception and feelings in other unrelated areas. This cognitive bias can lead to biased judgments, as positive attributes in one area are assumed to extend to other areas, even if there's no logical connection.

The *horn effect* suggests that individuals tend to form negative impressions of others based on a single negative trait or characteristic, often making snap judgments without considering other positive qualities or behaviors. This cognitive bias leads to an exaggeratedly negative view of the person or thing in question.

In perspective and in reference to Eve's irresistible emotional need to bite into the shiny red apple, don't live your life biting into Snow White's apple, meaning shiny but keeping your mind asleep. To fulfil my purpose at servicing the world and myself, I offer a fruitful pineapple, it's sweet inside, and packed with the full package of health benefits from the most valuable enzyme of all from this majestic fruit: Bromelain, and it's sweet for the brain.

Also in perspective, with the purpose of always showing up as your best self, for yourself when no one is watching, and sweetly good within is from the following suggested analogy: Once you go pineapple, you don't go back to apples.

What if your tool for peace in your mind, and for your inner warrior, is the one-off being *positively curious* with how tasty pineapple is, meaning taste before beauty? My observation with this pattern of our timeline speaks of a wise philosophic thought about life: Always cultivate yourself with principles, theories, and master them all but live like a common human. I apply this philosophy with my published work, meaning, I write for the common human with wise thoughts.

In life, you can't truly know unless – per one of the core fundamental anchors of my theory - you are *positively curious*, meaning not judging everything/everyone by their cover, or the critics. I mean, how is it truly possible to make a judgement without investigation? Like the exceptional pineapple history, which is yours to uncover with my book, *Worldwide fruitful travels with a pineapple,* you cannot know about a book's content unless you read it, and every new information becomes knowledge upgrading your perspective about yourself, and life, meaning that information nurtures transformation. This relates to people, the toilet with my peculiar book *The Toilet Theory*, and it also relates to the reading of a book, meaning go past the cover page, then pass the introduction. Since my Authorship journey in a world with likely more book titles than there are readers, I can't stress enough the pain I experience daily from the war at educating with the following: Always grow because you will never know enough, like what truly is between the cover & back page of The Pineapple Theory books.

Following my research about the pineapple, all analogies & metaphors created from absolutely anything & everything about the jewel of the jungle shared with my work (books, social media, mentorship, and more) are speaking to humans because it's about them. An example from the ongoing battle with pain and people's lack of *positive curiosity* can be shared because of what happened on November 2023 from my *guinea pig* experience, giving context to your reading, giving this book purpose, and my inner warrior was poked awake at remaining determined and resilient to life's adversity with a sweetheart. You see, it's not that life, the universe, or God wants to hurt you – sometimes - it simply need to teach you the hard way and this makes your inner warrior stronger at keeping yourself sweet. To achieve peace, we must face chaos, making pain worth something because it's a seed for growth.

At my third international book fair exhibit, the owner of a Canadian press agency, who was often avoiding and/or overlooking my work, was finally interested with admiration because I kept authentically showing up, and the brand finally got into them. An example of how pineapple my booth often looks like is as follows, and my guts are telling me that it's still not pineapple enough, meaning it's an opportunity for improvement. In life, there's no perfection, but you can achieve excellence.

The Pineapple Theory stand at the 2024 London book fair. Color imagery available with the title, Worldwide fruitful travels with a Pineapple.

Mexico – Guadalajara more precisely – is the host of an annual international book fair. Annually, the owner attends, and they wanted to present my books to three publishers. I gave them a copy of each book, and I waited for their return to follow up.

Post book fair, I received the feedback felt like asking to remove Harry Potter from Harry Potter, meaning, I was shared that the publishers would be interested if I remove, and I quote: *"the pineapple stuff!"*

Before letting my inner warrior unleash chaos like a provoked monkey, in life, always respond like a pineapple with *positive curiosity* and with the *3 wise pineapples.*

I had a call with them – the owner of the press agency - and learned that no one had read the books. The publishers looked at the cover page of each book, barely flipped the pages, and shared critics from what they didn't know and asked for, *"no pineapple stuff"*. What I personally found more spectacular about their request, is that Piña is *kinda* of a big deal in Mexico. In part, the city of Veracruz is referred to by the locals as, Pineapple Town or *Ch'uhuk Pina* in Spanish

We are talking about publishers here, people working in the book industry and not even reading an author's work. They exhibited the poor habits of seeking signs of a comfort zone, signs of boxed expectations, boxed patterns, and simply what's already popular to milk it. A problem from commercial publishers. That's everything my books are not, it is advertised early in each book they had on hand, and it explains why I promote my books as not being readers' typical books because they don't follow the standards, making them fruitfully authentic and organic in a mixed plate of fruit because I refuse to use A.I. when I write. It's also a perspective harvested from the blackbelt pineapple, living to its true self with courage and peace in its eyes in a world of standards but sadly, it disturbs and shocks many people.

Thanks to my inner warrior, always showing up with positivity and with confidence is a must, and from several experiences and new pains since my Authorship life, here's a brutal reality about the world of publishing because again, there are likely more titles than there are readers.

Publishing houses receives many manuscripts and 99% of submissions are rejected with most not being read. Meaning that in life, expect rejection and while many quit at the first handful of rejections, they let their self-confidence be stolen away by their own mind from how they choose to think and respond to each rejection. It's like a Post-Traumatic Shock Disorder (PTSD) and the suggested *Emotional Spider Web principle* from my theory. In perspective, for this situation following a few rejections, one will tell themselves, *"I won't be able to face another rejection."*

When there's rejection, it isn't time to dwell, retreat with yourself and your inner warrior meaning; step back, adjust, fix, improve, and march again forward. It's part of the process, it's the journey, and that's what cultivates you at achieving greatness from your excellence. In life, achieving your goals is not as important as what you become by achieving them and yes, working toward a purpose to serve the world truly is painful and it requires several sacrifices, and when there's no sacrifice to achieve, the purpose becomes the sacrifice.

Within and around, life feels like a battlefield, it's unfair and it will always be. Though, always show up with your ambitions and what is right to conquer yourself and the world, and it's never too late to march toward improvements in your life like with the following examples:

- Jan Koum started WhatsApp at 35.
- Asa Candler started Coca-Cola at 41.
- Sam Walton with Walmart at 44.
- Gordon with Starbucks at 51.
- Ferdinand with Porsche at 56.
- And Mr. Colonel Sanders who started KFC at 62.

But once you do engage with a first step forward, expect to hear the word *"no"* often. Yes, more than children who learned and realized what it means, and the effect *"no"* has on you. From what was once their dark side of the Moon, let's relate with the following list of people today shining following countless rejections because their inner warrior never surrendered with love and an inner roar:

- Albert Einstein was told he was slow and lacked talent for exact sciences.
- Walt Disney was fired because he apparently lacked imagination and had no good ideas.
- Oprah Winfrey was fired from her job as a television reporter because she was unfit for TV.
- Oscar-winning actor Sidney Poitier was told by a casting director: *"Why don't you stop wasting people's time and go out and become a dishwasher or something."*
- Muhammad Ali was told he was nothing more than a poor black person.
- Coco Chanel was told that a mere seamstress will never compete with the giants of fashion.
- Ferruccio Lamborghini was told that all he knew how to design is tractors.
- Thomas Edeson was told, *"you already failed 1,000 times, why keep going?"*
- Steven Spielberg got rejected from film school, 3 times.
- The Beatles were told they had no future in show business and that their guitar music was on the way out.

- Hugh Jackman was fired from 7-Eleven, as a cashier, for interacting too much with the customers.
- Elvis Presley got fired after his first performance.
- Coca-Cola sold only 25 bottles in the first year of business.
- Bill Gates showed his plan to 1,200 people, 900 said no (75%), 300 showed some interest (25%) for which 85 haven't done anything, 35 of those were serious, and 11 (1%) made him a billionaire.
- Steve Jobs, in 1985, was fired from Apple, a company he co-founded, and he returned in 1997 leading Apple to unprecedented success.
- Stephen King received 30 rejections for Carrie.
- Lastly, even J.K. Rowling's *Harry Potter and the Philosopher's Stone* was rejected 12 times by publishers before being welcomed by Bloomsbury. Just imagine how the 12 publishers must be holding their heads in shame today.

In life, if you wish to Thrive, you must know yourself to conquer yourself. Then, you'll conquer the world but remember that every time the world changed, it wasn't changed by those who had opinions, but by those who intuited what had to be done and they did it. Don't retreat, don't resign, don't stop. So, when I was told *"no pineapple stuff",* I leveraged the reality of the "beauty before taste" reality by updating this book's manuscript in 2025, and inside, I "stuffed" it with even more pineapples.

When Christopher Columbus brought the ananas back to Europe after being welcomed with the fruit in 1493 by the friendly inhabitants of the Antilles Island of Guadeloupe, it's no exaggeration to say that Europeans went bananas for this beautiful exotic fruit. Per my theory, when things are **B**ananas, remove the **B** and pineapple it will be!

As I was sharing, Europeans went bananas for the pineapple and a British colonist, Richard Ligon, who had a sugarcane plantation in Barbados, wrote at the time that the pineapple was, *'far beyond the choicest fruits of Europe'.*

When introduced to Britain in the 15th century, it became immediately clear that pineapples could not be cultivated in the unsuitable British climate. People still tried though, and for nearly two hundred years, there were many failed attempts to grow the fruit. Hot-Houses became the solution in the 18th century, and they made the pineapple become a fashionable commodity for the wealthy. Before that, pineapples had been successfully grown in mainland Europe in the late 16th century, yet still limited, and very expensive.

History suggests that Pieter de la Court developed greenhouse horticulture near Leiden from about 1658. Pineapple plants were distributed from the Netherlands to English gardeners in 1719 and French ones in 1730. I also found the following with my research:

In England, the first pineapple to have grown at Dorney Court, Dorney in Buckinghamshire, and a huge "pineapple stove" to heat the plants was built at the Chelsea Physic Garden in 1723. I also share in my books that urban legends dictate that Lambeth Bridge in London is a dedication to John Tradescant, who is said to have planted the first pineapple seed in London's soil. This fact exhibits today, at each corner of the bridge, pinecones on each monolith feeling like a pineapple memorial.

Copyright: Steve "Mr. Pineapple" Mathieu – Picture by HozzPhoto.com

In France, King Louis XV was presented with a pineapple that had been grown at Versailles in 1733.

In Russia, Peter the Great imported de le Court's method into St. Petersburg in the 1720s; in 1730, 20 pineapple saplings were transported from there to a greenhouse at Empress Anna's new Moscow palace.

Gardeners who were successful in growing pineapples were in high demand from the aristocracy who demanded pineapple all year round. Pineapple cultivation was big business, and contemporary gardeners published guides to building pineries and they shared tips on their achievements.

History suggests that the first pineapple propagated in Scotland is attributed to James Justice in 1728. Justice was a principal clerk of the Court of Session, but his passion for gardening resulted in a "garden paradise" created at Crighton House, just south of Edinburgh. Justice is said to be an innovator of growing pineapple methods, designing a pineapple stove designed to force the fruit.

In 1754, Justice shared his plan for the stove and other horticultural experiments in his publication *The Scots Gardiners Director,* and he also wrote further works on gardening in Britain. History also suggest that Justice was considered the father of Scottish gardening but his spending on his hobby – his passion - outweighed his income, and he acquired great debts. Justice died in 1763 and his accomplice, William Boucher of Comely Garden near Holyrood, was called upon to value Justice's Garden.

Somewhere between the early & mid-1900's, cultivating the fruit on home soil dwindled, as canned imports were readily available and a cheaper alternative than the time-consuming and expensive process of growing the fruit on home soil. The legacy of Scotland's love affair with the pineapple can still be admired at Dunmore, Stirlingshire the seat of John Murray, Earl of Dunmore.

2024 Dunmore Pineapple in Scotland - Copyright: Steve "Mr. Pineapple" Mathieu - Picture by Olga Tjukova.

Just as gardeners once defied climate to grow pineapples, we too must defy doubt to cultivate our purpose. In life, sometimes you lose and sometimes you win, like the following story from Taiwan.

Taiwan is one of the biggest pineapple exporters, it truly is big business for their economy, and the pineapple market is at the heart of a political war with China. DATA from 2021, according to Taiwan's Council of Agriculture, dictates that the island produces 420,000 tons of pineapple annually, and exported a little over 10% of that last year, with almost all of it going to China and it nurtured the political war harvesting the following movement when China blocked all exportations.

Without China's mainland sales, Taiwanese growers faced a possible glut of pineapples, and with it a danger that prices might fall.

President Tsai Ing-wen launched a *pineapple challenge* on social media with the purpose aimed at getting Taiwanese consumers to buy more of the fruit.

Taiwan's Foreign Minister used their Ministry's Twitter account (today X) to quote, *"urge like-minded friends around the globe to stand with #Taiwan & rally behind the #FreedomPineapple".*

The embassies of the US and Canada in Taiwan were "pineHapply" to oblige.

The American Institute in Taiwan posted several pictures to its social media page, including one of its directors with three pineapples on their desk.

The Canadian Trade Office in Taipei posted a photo of staff posing around a pineapple pizza, with a polite reminder that it was Canada's idea rather than Hawaii's. *"We, in the Canadian Office, like pineapples on pizza, especially pineapples from Taiwan!"* the post said.

When I published my pineapple research with my book, *Worldwide fruitful travels with a pineapple*, I shared the following pineapple fun fact about taking risk can be sweet in life and explaining why – not limited to - I traveled to Athens, Greece, in July 2022.

"The one who took the brave decision back in the 1960's to add pineapple to a pizza was a Greek immigrant to Canada. Responsible for this gastronomic innovation was none other than Sotirios "Sam" Panopoulos. (…)"

Within just a few days, the Taiwanese government's campaign led to enough orders to cover the pineapples that would have been exported to China.

With the purpose of uncovering "why" I chose the pineapple fruit for my theory, my 5-year in the making book project, *Worldwide fruitful travels with a pineapple*, is a must read because absolutely anything & everything about the pineapple is shared. Including both Scotland and Taiwan you have just read; there are several pineapple love stories from our history for which people had an inner roar to protect their love for the fruit. Even my story since I first published speaks of my inner roar.

Your inner roar is giving purpose to your inner warrior, and it has deep roots. It's almost inherited … or could it simply be our *amygdala* defending our *Ikea Effect* … or both! Nevertheless, an inner roar is an important symbol for several cultures for generations. For example:

In the Indian culture: The Tiger is a symbol of bravery, strength, power, and valor. Also, the Tiger symbolism is quite deep and varies from culture to culture. In most cases though, it is symbolic of strength.

Dragons in the Chinese culture symbolizes great power, good luck, and strength.

The Kangaroo in the Australian culture is symbolic of courage and energy, but also stamina.

Believe it because it's true, even the salmon exhibit an inner roar, and I refer to it as: The determination of a salmon!

2021 Vancouver Aquarium – Copyright & Picture by: Steve "Mr. Pineapple" Mathieu

The salmon. That one fish swimming counterflow to achieve a positive purpose, and it speaks volumes about humans because there are many salmons who counterflow a mass of followers:

- Fresh and new approaches to positively interact with others.
- There are no problems, only solutions.
- Biases kept under control.
- Master the art of managing positive emotions.
- Master the art of being positively curious.
- Master the art of time management.
- Easily moves on.
- Self-aware and self-reflective.
- See the big picture from an eagle view, other times from space.
- Visionary.
- And more.

The above are only a few examples of what defines a human with the determination of a salmon, and here's a suggested extrapolation. If we follow the *Pareto principle*, there is likely 20% of humans with the determination of a salmon who consistently counterflow the remaining 80%. Often, the one with the determination of a salmon is alone and it is challenging to positively manage their emotions. Furthermore, there are bears on the side trying to remove the salmon from its positive purpose. Other times, it's the *false positive* – the fisherman for this example – who will try to emotionally trick the salmon.

The determined salmon is often a free thinker. It will always seem crazy for those who don't take the time to *be positively curious.* The determined salmon will never apologize for evolving past the bear and emotional fisherman's comfort zone.

Somehow, when the determined salmon reaches its purpose, everyone loves the taste of what was offered & served since the start of its journey. All this time, there was nothing fishy about it!

The inspiration reminds us of the following: Never limit your ambitions because if you know your WHY, it means that you can see it - believe it – and achieve it. Believe to achieve. Here's a *guinea pig* story about this:

Several years ago, at a time when I never had the thought about becoming an author, I committed to something with myself. Ignorant to what was in the queue, it taught me the *extreme obvious* about what our inner warrior's inner roar is, and how it moves us to achieve humble victory with our inner battles. When I recount this story, as an author and following my research, wise voices from our past are whispering the importance of listening about ways of thinking to move ourselves, ways of seeing life, and that's exactly the refreshing purpose about what I wish to fruitfully inspire with The Pineapple Theory but also, I wish to inspire people to honor their word – it's not only rare, but honorable. Here's the story.

The Marathon

Running your life. Running with work for a corporate company. Running your own business. They feel like running a Marathon.

It starts with a purpose. It triggers an ambition. It is followed by ups & downs. It ends with an accomplishment.

It was the year 2010. I was at the restaurant with friends to recognize a friend's accomplishment. She had just completed the Montreal Marathon. She was inspired to do so. It inspired me and all eyes looked at me when I declared:

"Next year, we will all be here again at this table for the same reason we are here today. Why? Because I will be running the marathon."

Back in 2010, except for running to the toilet, I had never really run before. My friend's inspiration inspired me. It triggered a purpose in me. My new purpose triggered my ambition:

<u>The Ambition principle</u>

Socrates
Let he who would move the world first move himself.

Dalai Lama
With realization of one's own potential and self-confidence in one's ability; one can build a better world.

Steve Jobs
The people who are crazy enough to think they can change the world are the ones who do.

Richard Branson
There is no greater thing you can do with your life and your work than follow your passions. In a way that serves the world and you.

I was committed to getting out of my comfort zone which would allow me to discover myself more and conquer myself. I was committed to moving myself and building something better within me, no matter what other's thoughts. Often, the one sharing their ambition with others will receive one of the three following reactions:

They'll think it will be a failure.
They'll doubt.
They'll believe and support.

The no limit principle

Albert Einstein
Once we accept our limits, we go beyond them.

Bruce Lee
If you always put limits on everything you do - physical or anything else – It will spread into your work and into your life. There are no limits. There are only plateaus, and you must not stay there, you must go beyond them.

Les Brown
Life has no limitations; except the ones you make.

Nearly one year has passed. It was 23 September 2011. We were approximately 2,678 ambitious runners from various ages, various experiences. We were all on the Montreal Jacques-Cartier's Bridge, cheering each other. It was like putting fuel in everyone's energy tank as we were waiting for the green light.

4 hours 12 minutes
Was the approximate average time for the 2,678 ambitious runners to cross the finish line.

4 hours 12 minutes
With Ups and Downs.

4 hours 12 minutes
With yourself – with your mind – with your thoughts.

4 hours 12 minutes
Of what appeared to be a lifetime journey.

4 hours 12 minutes
It is a long run to the toilet!

When running in life, work, or in business, there are several Ups & Downs. When going down, the negative thoughts are attacking, and their attempts is to convince you and your inner warrior to surrender the war.

"Why am I doing this?"
"Why run, just walk!"
"You won't make it, just stop it!"

In life, you will never speak to anyone than you speak to yourself in your head, therefore, it is important to be kind to yourself.

The No Pain No Gain principle

Albert Einstein
Great spirits have always encountered violent opposition from mediocre minds.

Bruce Lee
Do not pray for an easy life, pray for the strength to endure a difficult one.

Steve Jobs
Sometimes life hits you on the head with a brick. Don't lose faith.

When you're down, it is like a superhero movie. The hero throughout its fight with the bad is down, breathing heavily, thinking they have been defeated, thinking it's over. That is until the hero looks back at their foundation and finds that tool and solution within to stand up and go back out there to accomplish its purpose.

The never quit principle

Buddha
The one in whom no longer exist the craving and thirst that perpetuate becoming; how could you track that awakened one, trackless, and limitless range.

Mohammad Iqbal
Failure is not fatal until we surrender trying again is the key to glorious victory.

Albert Einstein
You only fail when you stop trying.

Bruce Lee
Defeat is not defeat, unless accepted as a reality in your own mind.

Throughout the 4 hours 12 minutes journey of Ups and Downs, *The Never Quit Principle* is assisted by more powerful tools such as the following by The Pineapple Theory:

We all have emotional batteries. We are all energy. Your positive energy can help someone else recharge.

What starts with you is not about you, and because the best way to cheer yourself is to cheer somebody else up, I was that runner cheering all the other ambitious runners passing by me. I was giving them my positive energy even if I needed to receive some.

Unless you do the right things, the right things will not happen to you. Supporters at a Marathon, they applause, they express motivating words, and more. They were graciously sharing their positive energy to all 2,678 ambitious runners.

I remember throughout the 4 hours 12 minutes, when I was feeling down, my negative thoughts were trying to convince me to take a break from running and simply walking. The negative thoughts were running faster in my mind than I was physically.

That was until I recognized on the sidelines with its camera pointed at me, someone I know. He expressed supportive words, he took a shot, and it gave me a positive push to keep on going.

2011 Montreal Marathon - Copyright – Steve "Mr. Pineapple" Mathieu - Picture by Patrick Gauvin

4 hours 12 minutes
Of giving myself small challenges to give myself small recognition.

4 hours 12 minutes
On the clock when I crossed the finish line.

In a humble way, that feeling of accomplishment, this humble victory, rises to the eyes.

The self-recognition principle

Albert Einstein
The best way to cheer yourself is to cheer somebody else up.

Sadhguru
The most beautiful moments in life are moments when you are expressing your joy,

not when you are seeking it.

What started from someone's inspiration inspired me. One year later, we were all gathered to recognize an accomplishment. An accomplishment that inspired someone else. And the *pattern effect* – the cycle – initiated itself again:

A purpose is born - It triggers ambition - There's several Ups & Downs - And it ends with an accomplishment.

In life, you choose who you choose to be, and nobody else can do it for you. It all starts with a foundation. And you are your own foundation.

The Ambition Principle
The No Limit Principle
The No Pain No Gain Principle
The Self-Recognition Principle

They are tools available that can be part of your foundation, resonate in your temple defined as your mind, and become an example of how quotes of wisdom from our timeline can passionately move one forward in life. And your foundation, it is important to always work on it, which will make it better, always stronger. It requires practice and to always keep practicing. Today at home, I have my marathon jersey and medal.

2 objects
To remind me of an accomplishment when I feel down.

2 objects
To remind myself of several important pieces of my foundation.

2 objects
That reminds me to keep moving in life, no matter what.

And one of several mindsets to face life's challenge is like a warrior with a pineapple heart.

No Pain No Gain
Believe to Achieve
Don't Fear
Strong Mind
No Regrets
Focus

A fun fact about a marathon and a pineapple, being just one more thing exhibiting why the pineapple is a thriving choice of excellence for my theory, is inspired by an Israeli.

Moshe Lederfien from Israel runs marathons…while balancing a pineapple on his head! Lederfien ran 12 marathons with a pineapple on his head. The *pineapple marathoner* or the *pineapple marathon runner* served for Israel during the Yom Kippur War in 1973 and began running marathons at age 53. Lederfein never thought he could run, as he suffered from diabetes and high blood pressure. With his pineapple love, his inner roar also moved him.

Lederfien 12th marathon with a pineapple in Berlin, 2018 - Picture source: runingmagazine.ca

In life, when you love and are passionate about what you do, and "why" you do it, you become unstoppable. If you want to live a life most people don't, my question to you is, are you ready to do what most people don't?

No one can change your life other than you because no one is coming to save you. Don't wait for life to change you because life is the one waiting for you to change. The world may reject your fruit. But when you roar with love, resilience, and authenticity, you become the pineapple they never saw coming. Just like Columbus did. And it changed the world.

10

My wishes to you

This is my DNA — one of my life and leadership philosophies. The truth about me is simple: I never fake care for anyone. When I choose to care, it's real, it's genuine, and it's because I want to. Not because I expect anything in return, other than a better tomorrow inspired by the knowledge that everyone carries within, a sleeping seed for greatness.

I don't need validation to feel that what I'm doing is worthwhile. I see a target that no one else sees, and that's enough. What I give, I give from my heart, without hidden motives, without strings attached. I give because life must be lived for the honest happiness of others. I give deeply from my pineapple heart.

I believe in sincerity, integrity, loyalty, and in showing up for people simply because it's the right thing to do. That's who I am. That's how I cultivate a thriving pineHapply life, together.

If I invest my time, my energy, or my love, it's because you matter to me. Plain and simple. I don't play games or pretend to care. My feelings are honest. My kindness is real. And I believe kindness makes life more fruitful. My actions come from true intention. So, when I show up for you, when I offer support or encouragement, know that it's real. I'm there because I care. That's the kind of person I am, and that's how I choose to live.

My wish is for you to find happiness in your own way of thinking. And if it turns out I've slightly contributed to that, I'm honored. That's what I've been laboring toward since 2020. In a world with more book titles than readers, your review is a tap on the shoulder, a welcome as warm and sweet as a pineapple.

I wish you give yourself the love and care you deserve. That you invest in yourself, because you are your greatest worth. I wish for you to thrive with your mind. Every time you move with your heart, you need your mind. And when you wonder, you must know where your mind stands.

You see, you are important to me. That's why I do what I do with my pineapples, for you, even if you never asked for it. Because many answers in life are found in places, we haven't thought of looking at. I've stopped counting my sleepless nights. I've cried in the rain so you wouldn't see my pain toward society. And yet, I wake up every morning with ambition to serve people a zest of freshness in their day. To offer a touch of life. To help others thrive with pineHappliness.

Life can be tough. Life can be unfair. Sometimes we forget to prioritize ourselves, to recognize our worth. So, I remind you: take care of yourself. You deserve all the pineHappliness and peace the world has to offer. Be at peace with the world within, and you'll be at peace with the world around. Become what the world has to offer, that's your gift. Cultivate it. Protect it. Everybody needs it.

Maybe I was never part of your life. Maybe I'm not anymore. Maybe I am, for now. It doesn't change how I care for you. I just want you to be happy, to thrive, and to be in control of your life and mind. Through *The Pineapple Theory*, I want you to be pineHapply, to be the positive solution that you are. And to find balance, even if a pineapple doesn't stand perfectly straight. That's the truth about life: it's not emotionally perfect, but it still stands making all other fruits look more vibrant when served on a mixed plate.

Even if we're not together, what if we are? Books are the geometry of one soul reaching another. Each book lives hundreds of lives. Dare to open many and keep your mind wide open to the world and to yourself.

I may never experience the true success of *The Pineapple Theory*. Only when I pass — empty-handed, as I entered life — will it become successful. And knowing this means I've understood one of life's meanings.

The philosophy behind my quotation is this: The one who plants a seed knows they will likely never sit in the shade of its tree. It starts with you — because it's not about you. In perspective, *The Pineapple Theory* book series are seeds. And you, the reader, are the continuum. You bloom from your reading. And the tree grows.

Old Frankfurt (DE) 2022 – Copyright Steve "Mr. Pineapple" Mathieu Photographer: Marc Maria

Sweetly yours, Mr. Pineapple

Montreal (CA-QC) 2021 – Copyright Steve "Mr. Pineapple" Mathieu Photographer: Anthony Scorroco

Much of what is called "personal choice" is, in fact, pre-scripted behavior. From childhood onward, individuals absorb cultural templates for what constitutes a successful life. Templates that include educational milestones, career trajectories, lifestyle markers, and relationship norms. These scripts are rarely questioned, because they are embedded before the capacity for critical reflection fully develops.

Psychologically, this phenomenon is known as *Path Dependency* (David, 1985). The brain, like any efficient system, tends to follow previously established tracks, not because they are optimal, but because they are familiar, socially rewarded, and cognitively economical. The path of least resistance becomes the default, reinforced by repetition and approval. It is comfort in a highly inflammable fabric.

This internalized blueprint is further cemented by *Normative Conformity* and *Social Conditioning* (Asch, 1956). Individuals pursue status symbols — degrees, titles, salaries — not necessarily because these goals align with their intrinsic values, but because they are validated by their peer group. The brain responds with dopamine, a neurochemical reward for social acceptance. But the effect is fleeting. The deeper psychological need for meaning remains unmet.

This is why so many people experience chronic dissatisfaction despite visible success. Their lives are optimized for external validation rather than internal coherence. Over time, this misalignment can lead to *Existential Dissonance*, a psychological tension between one's actions and one's authentic values.

The way forward begins with *Radical Self-Inquiry*. In clinical practice, this resembles the first phase of *Schema Therapy*, where individuals identify core beliefs and behavioral patterns inherited from early life experiences. Readers can begin by asking:

- Which aspects of my life feel truly mine?
- Which goals energize me, and which drain me?
- What must I give up to become who I wish to become?

Writing these reflections down is not just cathartic, it activates *Metacognition*, the ability to think about one's own thinking, which is essential for change.

Next comes *Cognitive Restructuring*, a technique from CBT. This involves challenging automatic thoughts and reframing inherited beliefs. For example, "Success means having a high-status job" can be re-evaluated as "Success means living in alignment with my values."

Then, *Value Reconstruction* begins, the deliberate rebuilding of one's life from the inside out. This mirrors the principles of *Narrative Psychology*, where individuals re-author their personal story by choosing new meanings and directions. The goal is not to erase the past, but to reinterpret it in a way that empowers future choices.

True fulfillment is not found in conformity, but in alignment, where behavior reflects belief, and goals emerge from within rather than being imposed from without.

There's much more to it than psychological concepts. When interacting with people, I saw how fear of failure and external judgment held them back. I experienced this myself. And yet, I moved forward. I took one step, and that step became thousands. That's the path. And it mirrors the story of pineapple cultivation in 16th-century Britain, where the climate was unfit to grow this royal fruit. Yet they tried. They built greenhouses. They failed. And they kept going.

The reason many don't dare - or feel like nothing they do works - is because they're chasing quality instead of quantity. But quality is a byproduct of quantity.

Everyone wants to be good without going through being bad. They disguise failure as identity. They think if they plan hard enough, they can avoid mistakes. But the truth is: the first 50, 100, maybe even 500 attempts will suck.

There's a famous study: one group was told to make the perfect clay pot; the other, to make as many as possible. The second group ended up creating better pots. Why? Because while the first group theorized, the second group learned by doing. This applies to writing, editing, design, business — anything. If you only aim for quality, you overthink, you stall, and you put nothing out. Quantity gives you feedback. Feedback creates growth. Growth leads to quality.

That's what I share with readers and mentees, a lesson I carried home from Athens: Stop asking if what you're doing is good enough. Just do it. Without expectation. Just produce. And you'll reach a quality you couldn't have reached by chasing it. Because the fastest way to become successful at anything is to be unsuccessful, as fast and as often as needed.

A valuable lesson from Marvel's 2022 movie Wakanda Forever, is that Princess Shuri (the Black Panther) failed several times before successfully creating the infamous herb. She kept trying; volume became quality.

My story about The Pineapple Theory is nothing short about this. Anything & everything about The Pineapple Theory is 100% human made. So, yes, it failed several times before being able to offer a savory product. Although I do not have "status symbols", I invested in myself, and my purpose, by traveling the world to ensure accuracy with my research, truly feel the experience to speak from the heart about it, and the work does not fail. In fact, Tim Denning, a writer and entrepreneur who champions self-education. He wrote: *"Never underestimate someone who practices self-education in their free time."*

His message highlights how self-educators often quietly build mastery, resilience, and insight without fanfare or formal credentials. It's a reminder that the most dangerous minds aren't always found in classrooms, they're found in curiosity. With my theory, I suggest 15 fundamental anchors define as the roots of a pineapple, and one of the 3 cores fundamental anchors is a real game changer called, *be positively curious.*

So, what if you could uncover more of my titles? They cultivate the best version of yourself with a creatively sweet balance of biography for inspiration, psychology for understanding, philosophy for perspectives, science for curiosity, fiction for creativity, and self-help for action.

Together, they introduce refreshing new ways of thinking and juicy new ways of seeing life. You'll study yourself sincerely because awareness is a rare treasure. And it fuels long-term thinking.

As mentioned, they are 100% human made with real travels for 100% organic experiences. I travel the world to write my books, and I carefully observed tens of thousands of years across our timeline to identify fundamental emotional patterns, then I blended the ananas into the recipe.

It was a pleasure hosting you in the Universe of *The Pineapple Theory*. Keep reading. Keep growing. Keep expanding.

Let the fruit speak.

Cooking - History - Health Benefits
Travel Activities - and the ultimate proof that
life & humans are amazingly pineapple
WORLDWIDE
FRUITFUL
TRAVELS
WITH A
PINEAPPLE
UNITED KINGDOM
IMMIGRATION OFFICER
LONDON
ARRIVAL
approved
Mr. Pineapple

Discover the art of positive affirmation, positive persuasion, and thinking without emotional conflict.
FEEL & THINK
LIKE A
PINEAPPLE
Mr. Pineapple

Earn their heart first, then,
everything else with your life &
leadership entreprenurial mindset.
MARKET & SELL
YOURSELF,
PRODUCTS,
SERVICES
LIKE A
PINEAPPLE
Mr. Pineapple

The Legend of the Thousand Eyes
PiNa the AnaNas
MR. PiNEAPPLE
PiNa the AnaNas
and The
3 Legend of the Wise Pineapples
MR. PiNEAPPLE

Become #1 when making #2s!
A life & toilet book about life & toilets is brilliantly perfect & the most peculiar toilet book reading ever.
THE TOILET THEORY
Steve "Mr. Pineapple" Mathieu

Printed in Dunstable, United Kingdom

80082493R00127